Stories from the Edge

A Theology of Grief

Greg Garrett

Westminster John Knox Press
LOUISVILLE • LONDON

Unless otherwise indicated, Scripture quotations, are from the New Revised Standard Version of the Bible, copyright © 1989 by the Division of Christian Education of the National Council of the Churches of Christ in the U.S.A. and used by permission.

Scripture quotations marked NJB are from *The New Jerusalem Bible*, copyright © 1985 by Darton, Longman & Todd, Ltd., and Doubleday, a division of Bantam Doubleday Dell Publishing Group, Inc. Reprinted by permission of the publisher(s).

Book design by Sharon Adams
Cover design by Pam Poll Graphic Design
Cover photo: © Alan Powdrill/Getty Images

First edition
Published by Westminster John Knox Press
Louisville, Kentucky

This book is printed on acid-free paper that meets the American National Standards Institute Z39.48 standard. ♾

PRINTED IN THE UNITED STATES OF AMERICA

08 09 10 11 12 13 14 15 16 17 — 10 9 8 7 6 5 4 3 2 1

Library of Congress Cataloging-in-Publication Data

Garrett, Greg.
    Stories from the edge : a theology of grief / by Greg Garrett.
        p. cm.
    ISBN 978-0-664-23204-7 (alk. paper)
    1. Grief—Religious aspects—Christianity.   I. Title.
    BV4905.3.G38 2008
    248.8'66—dc22

                                                2008002519

For my rector and friend the Rev. David Boyd,
who has experienced grief,
but embraces hope

Contents

Draw your chair up close to the edge of the precipice and I'll tell you a story.

F. Scott Fitzgerald, *Notebooks*

Introduction

When we find a difficulty, we may always expect that a discovery awaits us.

C. S. Lewis, *Reflections on the Psalms*

A Difficulty

Although Mrs. Gonzales was sitting with her family outside in the
sixth-floor waiting room, you could hear her wailing throughout
the sixth floor whenever the outer doors to the Medical Intensive
Care Unit (MICU) opened.[1] Maybe that's the practical reason
explaining why the sixth-floor caseworker asked me to speak with
her: her keening, her calls for her son Hector, her continuing
groans of "Why? Why?" might have been audible and even disturbing to some of the patients fighting for life. Or maybe she
thought they might load additional stress on some of the family
and friends of other patients who themselves were at or near their
own breaking points.

But it's also possible that the caseworker asked me to talk with
Mrs. Gonzales simply because she was so clearly a person in pain.
The source of her anguish was readily apparent: her Hector lay in a
bed in the MICU, where his body, ravaged by alcohol and drug use,
was failing him, one system after another. He was still a relatively

young man, forty-six, and his rapid collapse must have been traumatic to all of those who loved him.

It was obviously traumatic to her.

As floor chaplain, it was my job to be present with people like Hector and his mother as they were in the midst of suffering, so it would have been my task and my privilege to sit with Mrs. Gonzales no matter what reason prompted the caseworker to send me to her. After getting some details on Hector's case from his nurse, I passed through the MICU toward the waiting area, the glass-walled rooms containing seriously ill patients on my right as I walked. When I pushed open the door to the waiting room, and heard Mrs. Gonzales's anguished call, "Hector! My son!" I breathed a prayer from Psalm 23 I used often that summer before I entered a hospital room or confronted a difficult situation: "Yea, though I walk through the valley of the shadow of death I will fear no evil."

In the waiting room I found Mrs. Gonzales easily. She was a short, weeping woman in her sixties, seated against one of the walls, surrounded by her family, Hector's children, and his ex-wife. I walked over to her, put my hand on her shoulder, and introduced myself. Then I told her, "I heard that you've just gotten some very hard news, and I've come to be with you."

She looked up at me, registered my presence and my identity, and then, looking me in the eyes as though I might have an answer, let out another broken-hearted cry: "Why, God? Why?"

I nodded my head in sympathy, because I felt her anguish strongly. But there was no good response to her question. Or, at least, there was no easy answer I could give, no immediate panacea I could offer, and I had learned better than to try. She would have to earn her own answer.

Only then could her story be complete.

All I could tell her in that moment was, "I'm sorry," and all I could offer her was my presence, my willingness to stand alongside her in her suffering as a representative of the most high and holy God.

Often that was enough.

I met Mrs. Gonzales and many of the other people who populate this book during the summer of 2006 when I was a seminarian working full-time as a chaplain intern at Brackenridge Hospital, the regional trauma center located in my hometown of Austin, Texas. Although our name badges called us interns, we had every duty given to the staff chaplains except for the sacramental duties set aside for the Catholic priests. During those twelve weeks that I was enrolled in Clinical Pastoral Education (CPE), I worked in-house at Brackenridge Hospital every day, visiting patients and working with the staff in the emergency room, in intensive care, and on a "regular" hospital floor where cases were acute but not critical. I also rotated through regular nights and weekend shifts on call when I served Brackenridge and four other Austin hospitals operated by the Seton Hospital system as lead chaplain, responding to any spiritual emergency in the Seton system, whether heart attack, car crash, frightening diagnosis, or requests for prayer.

As part of the CPE process, I also met for three hours three times a week with a group of six peers and our CPE supervisor, Cyd, to discuss with them what I was seeing, feeling, thinking about—the things we all were wrestling with during this experience of chaplaincy.

This last made my chaplaincy more than just a blur of images, voices, and pain: it also began to make some sense of what I was experiencing in patients' rooms and with their families and friends in halls and waiting areas. This was perhaps the first time in my life that I had been invited—nay, required—to try to process what I was feeling as I was feeling it, and it was vital, because what I was experiencing was far outside the middle-class world I normally inhabited.

Although I have lived a life that has taught me plenty about pain and suffering, I had never experienced the kind of unexpected trauma—and the results of it—that I observed and hoped to soothe that summer. Since Brackenridge was a regional trauma center, we were a magnet for accidents, shootings, drownings—all sorts of immediate and unforeseen suffering. My patients, their loved ones, and our staff were confronted by problems that sometimes seemed to have come out of thin air. Mrs. Gonzales, for example—in the moment after she met me and asked why God was doing this—confided to me, "Hector was getting better. He went to mass with me on Sunday."

For her, as for many of those whom I met that summer, her son's sudden illness and impending death made no sense, and that, perhaps more than anything, was what she was wrestling with, the collapse of the world of stories she had lived inside.

During the summer, I heard the stories of many people like Mrs. Gonzales who suddenly found themselves in places of suffering, loss, or mourning: Michael, a fifteen-year-old boy shot in the back because (he said) he had tried to bum cigarettes off the wrong guy; the mother and brother of Lewis, a thirty-five-year-old ex-con, who told me that they had not even known Lewis was out of prison and back in town until the Brackenridge Hospital social worker located them and notified them that Lewis was dying in the Intensive Care Unit of liver and kidney failure; the family and fiancé of Amanda, a beautiful twenty-one-year-old girl badly injured in a motor vehicle accident, who came up to the hospital faithfully and remained hopeful although Amanda never regained consciousness during all my weeks as chaplain on her floor; Carina, the young mother of a seventeen-year-old boy with Down's syndrome, who had turned her back on him for only a moment, but during that moment he had fallen into the lake, drowned, and subsequently been revived and brought to Brackenridge; Howard, an eighty-seven-year-old man with a couple of months left on a terminal diagnosis of lung cancer, who wanted to know what God was really like, and who asked me flat out if God would mind if we prayed for a miracle.

These people, the others I encountered, and I myself, in my own times of loss and pain—all of us were very much alike. In the face of our loss, we were shaken, and the stories that we lived by were failing us because they could not make room for what was happening to us. This shouldn't surprise anyone. Rabbi Harold Kushner, author of perhaps the best-known (and still one of the most useful) books about God and suffering, *When Bad Things Happen to Good People*, wrote that book out of the soul pain and confusion he felt at the slow deterioration and death of his young son Aaron. Rabbi Kushner described that work as "a very personal book, written by someone who believes in God and in the goodness of the world, someone who has spent most of his life trying to help other people believe, and was compelled by a personal tragedy to rethink everything he had been taught about God and God's ways."[2] In Rabbi Kushner's case, the stories of God he had been taught and had taught others about how they might conduct their lives suddenly shattered against the rock face of unfairness. As Kushner put it, "If God existed, if He was minimally fair, let alone loving and forgiving, how could He do this to me?"[3] I discovered this pattern of disillusionment—and the resulting questions—over and over again in the hospital, and have come to recognize them as they occur in the lives of those who suffer.

Even C. S. Lewis, the writer I quoted at the head of this introduction, who could speak so beautifully about the opportunities awaiting us in every difficulty—a popular theologian and Christian apologist who could write a best-selling defense of suffering, *The Problem of Pain*—even this giant of the faith wrote, in the wake of his beloved wife's death:

> Meanwhile, where is God? . . . Go to him when your need is desperate, when all other hope is vain, and what do you find? A door slammed in your face, and a sound of bolting and double bolting on the inside. After that, silence. You may as well turn away. The longer you wait, the more emphatic the silence will become. There are no lights in the windows. It might be an empty house. Was it ever inhabited?[4]

When our stories collapse, one thing that can happen when we stand outside the door knocking is that we can know despair. In response to one of the best-known stories in the Gospel of John, the raising of Lazarus, Robin Griffith-Jones writes of the twin responses the sisters Mary and Martha have to their brother Lazarus's death: "Martha's belief and Mary's despair: The two impulses are rarely separate at bereavement."[5] So it's fair to accept that these twin pulls toward both hope and despair are a natural part of the grieving process; it was Mrs. Gonzales's despair that caused her to wail and to weep.

But it was her hope—and her faith—that caused her to ask me, "Why?"

Of course, it is hope that we will hope for. A theological word we will sometimes encounter in our journey here is *eschatology*, a word that is often taken to refer to the end of the world, to what happens after we die, to the end of cosmic time. But I find myself very much drawn to the belief called *inaugurated eschatology*, a subset of this branch of theology that scientist/theologian John Polkinghorne defines as a balance between hope in what is to come someday in some end-time, and hope that God is transforming the world—and us, in it—right now, even as we speak.[6] It is perhaps the sort of thing that Jürgen Moltmann means when he says that those who follow the Christian hope look "for the coming of God's kingdom 'on earth as it is in heaven.'"[7]

So we will hope for hope. But it is despair we will have to confront in these stories, over and over again, because it is in the loss of meaning, the failure of our strongly held stories, that despair grows and groans.

As we prepare to wrestle with and read these stories, I should be clear about one thing from the outset of this book: while I was a good chaplain when the chips were down, I do not think of myself as the hero or even the subject of this book. Nor is it my intent in these pages to write a story about the life and work of a hospital chaplain (even though such a book might be of some interest and even of value, particularly if it were focused on people like the staff chaplains alongside whom it was my honor to work and learn).

Instead, this book is focused on the grief and suffering I witnessed (and on some that I have lived through), and on what a person like myself—a teacher, storyteller, and theologian—has learned about some of our most important faith questions as a result of inhabiting the roles of observer, comforter, and representative of the universal church in those moments of grief and suffering. A hospital is a sort of laboratory for the study of grief; it is a setting that can be hyper-realistic, dramatic, life with most of the boring parts taken out and more dramatic moments inserted. Whether we are talking about the loss of life, the loss of loved ones, or the loss of health and possibility, the stories that emerge from a hospital setting can crystallize questions that might take us decades to explore in the course of a relatively happy life: Where is God in the midst of suffering? How do people find strength, comfort, courage, and faith in the midst of terrible adversity like Mrs. Gonzales's pain? How can caregivers, family, and friends stand alongside such terrible suffering?

To explore those questions through the stories of people like Mrs. Gonzales and her family—to retell them, to think about them in such a way that others might benefit from them, and to consider how we might apply the collected wisdom from some of our faith, philosophical, and narrative traditions on grief and suffering—is the purpose of this book. While I will hardly be able to absent myself from these pages—my observations and conclusions are essential parts of this process, and as Henry David Thoreau said, I would hardly talk so much about myself if I knew anyone else as well—the stories of the suffering I encountered in the hospital will be our entry into exploration.

Because we are using story as our primary mode for considering the problem of pain, suffering, and meaning, this is a work of *narrative theology*. By that I mean that I will be telling and retelling stories, examining them for theological meaning (What can these stories tell us about God and our experience of God?), and sifting them for philosophical understanding (What wisdom can these stories give me about how I should live my life?). I have discovered that being able to put the pieces of our experiences together in some satisfactory way—telling a story that makes sense, if you will—is an essential part of the process of a meaningful life. The thing is, some of the stories we tell that make some sort of sense to us may be dangerous theologically, emotionally, spiritually. Believing that God is punishing you for your past sins by giving your son an incurable cancer may allow you to make some sort of sense out of the trauma your family is experiencing, but it seems to me that it is an unhealthy kind of sense—and probably an unhealthy story about who God is and how God participates in our lives.

Because we'll be forcibly interrogating some of the most common and widely held narratives, both sacred and secular, by which

Americans shape their experience, this book might rightfully be called postmodern. It's true that many of the so-called master narratives begin to leak when you fill them with grief, and pointing out their inadequacies in favor of individually constructed narratives fits in with many of the developments in postmodern thought. Following the example of Jean-François Lyotard and others, we will be expressing a healthy skepticism toward many meta-narratives.

But I'm also still modern enough to think there must be some overarching stories that hang together, some master narratives that feed our souls rather than falling apart in the face of trouble. My own experience indicates that being a person of faith requires our constant and vigilant work to reconcile the conflicts between one-size-fits-all belief and our own personal practice and understanding. Some stories must (and, I believe, do) mean something to many people—and still hold up under the pressure of our own individual narratives.

One afternoon in our group time, Cyd, our supervisor, told my colleagues and me that Mrs. Gonzales's question—"Why?"—is the question of all patients and those who love them (and perhaps of those who care for them as well). I believe that she was right, although that *why* often led people on to a whole lot of other disturbing questions: Why has this happened to me? Why did God cause this (or permit it)? Haven't I lived a good life? Aren't I a good person? Didn't I do everything that God required? Am I being punished? How am I going to get through this? Where is God when I need Him? Who or what is God, anyway?

I want to suggest, though, that first we step back from all of these questions—even from that initial *why*. Before we can fruitfully ask why suffering has entered our lives, first we should examine our core beliefs about God, about ourselves, and about life itself—to tell, hear, and understand our foundational narratives. Once we begin to see what stories we've accepted, we can better understand what underlies our painful questions about fairness, health, safety, and assurance that emerge when we experience suffering.

In our first chapters we'll explore some of the stories that shape our understanding of God and our relationship to God, as well as those stories that have grown up in our culture to shape our daily lives. You may be surprised to see what unexplored givens we have accepted equally about God, the omnipotence of medicine, our right to happiness, and our ability to purchase it.

We will then be following a narrative approach to suffering that will be less systematic than synthetic: with each chapter, we will unpack stories from my chaplaincy experience organized around a central idea, "read" them to glean their theological content, and seek life wisdom where we can find it in Scripture, wisdom traditions, and narrative. Some of these stories (and their corresponding wisdom) will complement those that have gone before; some may stand in tension with them. We will do the same with stories about suffering from the Bible and other wisdom traditions, from theologians and philosophers, and from literary and artistic sources.

By gathering and considering all of these stories about suffering, I think we will be able to do something similar to what the great American modernist poet Wallace Stevens did in his poem "Thirteen Ways of Looking at a Blackbird," or to what we do when we walk around a statue and look at it from all angles: by viewing it from a number of perspectives, we have a far greater chance of understanding the full scope of the object in view.

These stories of chaos should ultimately help bring us toward some notion of order. We will learn where we are.

And where we might be.

Later in his own experience of grief, C. S. Lewis wrote in a notebook that when he carried his questions about his wife's death and his pain to God, he still received no answer. But now he understood that it was a special kind of silence—not a locked door, as he had once written, but more like his coming under a silent and loving gaze, "As though [God] shook his head not in refusal but waiving the questions. Like, 'Peace, child; you don't understand.'"[8]

Maybe as we examine the stories we live by, we too will learn to ask better questions—or to come to a place where the answers matter less than we once believed.

✤✤✤✤✤✤✤✤

But this too is true—stories can save you.

Tim O'Brien, *The Things They Carried*

Stories—and Meanings

"There was a man—or woman—and . . ." This is story, or at least, the bare beginnings of one. Narrative at its most basic level works in this way: you have a *character* or characters to whom something happens. In a complete story, that action or event may be the beginnings of a *plot*, but it is important to realize that what defines plot is our ability to make sequential actions fit together in some logical fashion. English novelist E. M. Forster described it in this way: "The king died and the queen died" is a sequence of events, but it most assuredly is *not* plot; however, "the king died and the queen died of grief" *is*.[9]

It's the sequential and logical fitting together of parts that matters; Forster's example reminds us that we cannot form stories without being able to connect the dots. Character plus action do not equal a satisfactory narrative without a sense of underlying meaning. Plot typically moves from an initiating action through complications toward some sort of climax and ultimate resolution. The climax may be a physical action: a woman wins an election, a man escapes from prison. But in many of the stories we'll be telling (or retelling) here, the climax is emotional or spiritual rather than physical, although it may arise from drama-laden physical actions.

The events of these stories should lead us toward some sort of understanding, some sort of reflection that may bring us closer to enlightenment. The literary term we employ to name this enlightenment is *epiphany*. You may know that epiphany is not only a Greek word but also a word bearing religious associations. It means, literally, "showing forth" or revelation; in liturgical traditions, we celebrate the Feast of the Epiphany, the date on the sacred calendar when we commemorate the "showing forth" of the God-incarnate child Jesus to the wise men of the East. Epiphany is what we hope for when we listen to a story: insight, inspiration, some understanding that we did not possess before. We want to know why things happened. And we hope to learn what those happenings mean.

So our crash course in narrative has led us to meaning: we began with character and plot (perhaps leading to an epiphany), and at last we cast about for what literature teachers have always most loved, *theme*. What is this plot about characters truly *about*? What does it tell us about life? In words sometimes employed by teachers, "What is the author [or Author] trying to tell us in this story?"

It is in theme that we find ultimate meaning: When we read, hear, or live a story, we ultimately seek to know what the point of the story is. As Forster noted in distinguishing between a simple story and a sequential plot, "If it is in a story we say: 'And then?' If it is in a plot we say 'Why?'"[10] It is here that we come back to my supervisor's understanding of the patient's fundamental question: I am in this story where these things are happening, and I really want to know why they're happening.

Why?

Throughout the Synoptic Gospels (Matthew, Mark, and Luke), Jesus told stories: "There was a man—or a woman—who . . ." We know that people, sometimes great crowds of them, listened to the stories Jesus told. Sometimes the stories were clear enough that Jesus' rivals understood that he was attacking them through the medium of narrative, but we can also feel certain that sometimes people simply scratched their heads even after they had listened carefully. We know that because often someone (usually one of his rock-headed disciples themselves) asked Jesus to delineate the meaning—to explain the themes of the story, if you will—for them, as in this instance from the thirteenth chapter of the Gospel of Matthew:

> Jesus told the crowds all these things in parables; without a parable he told them nothing. This was to fulfill what had been spoken through the prophet: "I will open my mouth to speak in parables; I will proclaim what has been hidden from the foundation of the world."

> Then he left the crowds and went into the house. And his disciples approached him, saying, "Explain to us the parable of the weeds of the field." (Matt. 13:34–36)

Why did the disciples (and why do we) ask to have stories explained? Because lessons are typically rooted deep in stories, not floating for easy harvest on the surface: we experience the events of stories, but they are not systematic in the way they present the world. We have to create our own systems, our own meaning. As the early church (and the church ever since) could tell you, Jesus told stories, but you can't found a faith tradition simply on stories; they have to be sifted for meaning.

Why did these events happen? What am I supposed to do as a result of them? And what am I supposed to learn about God, existence, faith within them?

In the stories and the related discussions of grief we will consider here, meanings may sometimes be provisional; many of the people whose stories I stepped into in the hospitals during the summer were a long way away from coming to a complete understanding of their experiences, and even writing some time after the end of these events, I can't be confident that I fully understand their import. We grow in wisdom and understanding as we reflect, gain critical distance, tell our stories again and again.

But as Anne Lamott notes at the conclusion of one of her essays, sometimes provisional meanings have to be enough for people of faith: "This is plenty of miracle for me to rest in now," she says in response to the story unfolding in front of her, and she can take a step, and then another step with that assurance.[11]

Stories and their provisional meanings may also speak differently to different people. The words of wisdom spoken by the Desert Fathers were often intended to "diagnose" a specific spiritual and very individual ailment, and my friend Rodger Kamenetz says that in the Jewish rabbinic tradition, the great rabbis used to select stories to tell individuals based on what they specifically needed to hear to be healed.

Of course, a single story may not be sufficient to lead us to a common understanding of the experience of suffering, loss, and death. Jesus didn't tell a single story about the kingdom and stop there: "The kingdom of heaven is like this." He told a number of them, over and over: "The kingdom of heaven is like this. And this. And this."

So in this book, we too will consider a number of stories that say, "Suffering is like this. And this. And this."

Or "Suffering means this. And this. And this. And perhaps one of these is the story you need to hear to be healed."

It may not be a cure, precisely.

But, perhaps, a prescription for hope.

Within these pages—and with these pages—I hope that you will sift through stories of grief to discover at least one story that acknowledges the experience of suffering and that feels like a truth you can accept and make your own.

My very first day of CPE, I had to go to the sprawling Seton Medical Center to get my identity badge for the Seton system. As I wandered the maze of hallways in that hospital looking for the ID office, I got seriously lost, which I did nearly every time I went to Seton. That summer I had frequent nightmares about being lost in Seton Medical Center that were disturbingly similar to that first actual experience: Dead ends. Endless hallways. Unmarked doors.

Every time I went to Seton, I felt the need for a map—or bread crumbs.

But at last I found the personnel photo office, had my picture taken, emerged with the badge that would admit me to parking garages and emergency rooms throughout the Seton system, and threaded my way back to the entrance of the hospital.

There at the front door, I observed a new patient, an elderly woman on a gurney who was being wheeled into the hospital from an ambulance. Although this was not, apparently, an emergency, the woman lay atop the gurney, gray and drawn and clearly in distress as they began to process her for admission. The paramedic had stepped over to the volunteer station to ask a question of a red-vested volunteer at the desk, while others finished her paperwork.

Like his patient, the paramedic, too, apparently was suffering.

"Umm," I heard him say, fidgeting and blushing, "can you tell me how to get to the bathroom?"

Suddenly everything fell into place for me.

The Book of Common Prayer tells us that in the midst of life we are in death. But I believe it is also true that in the midst of death, life continues. What that means is that even when they are confronted by suffering and pain, people still seek directions through the maze—and not just directions to the bathroom.

What we will hope to do in this book is to uncover some directions—maybe not a one-size-fits-all set leading everyone inexorably to the same destination, but at the very least a compass heading for the perplexed. In the exploration, I hope to help people make meaning out of pain, develop their own working theology of suffering, and help those who experience suffering, whether directly or as caregivers and comforters. And in this exploration, I hope we will find ourselves—and perhaps even something outside ourselves—in ways we never have before.

Chapter One

"Why, God, Why?"

Stories of God

God created order out of disorder, cosmos out of chaos, and God can do so always, can do so now.
Archbishop Desmond Tutu, *God Has a Dream:*
A Vision of Hope for Our Time

Belief in God—But What God?

Some of my colleagues at Baylor University recently released a milestone study about Christian faith and practice in America in which they discovered, to no one's surprise, that a vast majority of Americans believe in God. That statistic is where most studies in the past have stopped, satisfied with their results. But this new Baylor study went a crucial step further. It asked respondents, When you say you believe in God, what do you mean? What is your understanding of this God in whom you believe?

And the results were startling. Yes, the vast majority of Americans believe in God. But the study revealed that Americans had different ideas of God in mind when they told the surveyor that they believe in God. Some Americans, for example, believe in a vengeful God who is closely involved in the affairs of humankind; some believe in a God who has little connection with earthly affairs and will judge humankind at the

1

end of time (as in that eschatology thing we talked about in the introduction).

What the study discovered is that participants' images of God had a strong correlation to other sections of their life, such as whether they were more likely to vote Republican or Democrat, whether they were more or less likely to support the death penalty, how often they attended church, whether they believed the Bible was the literal or figural word of God.[1]

Taking a page from their playbook, I want to argue that a person's conception of God also affects her or his understanding of grief and suffering. How can it not? The story that people tell about God will determine whether they believe God intervenes miraculously in human affairs, whether they believe God is loving or vengeful, whether they believe God has power over sickness and death. Whether those beliefs are closely examined or not, whether they are conservative literalist stories or liberal symbolic understandings, all persons have what John Dominic Crossan calls an "operative theology" in which they apply their beliefs about God.[2] And in the hospital setting, as well as in my own experience of grief, I found that it was vital to understand who God is (or who we think God is) so that we could understand how that version of God might or might not work in a given situation.

On the Friday morning of my second full week as a chaplain at Brackenridge, I faced my first rotation through the Brackenridge and Austin Children's Hospital emergency rooms as ER chaplain. All of the chaplain interns were assigned one morning a week in ER; we also regularly went to ERs and ICUs across Austin when we were on call.

My staff chaplain mentor, Pablo Holguin, had taken me around the ER earlier in the week and introduced me to the nurses, social workers, and other staff bustling around. He also introduced me to an ER doctor or two, but I had almost no contact with doctors that summer; nurses, techs, caseworkers, and social workers were typically my hospital lifeline, the people who called me for help, the people who told me what I needed to know about the patients.

I used my still-sparkling-new employee badge to let myself in the backdoor of the ER, the automatic doors swinging slowly out to admit me. Then I walked through the emergency room and poked my head out the front door to check out the desk and waiting area. A number of people were already in the waiting room; three ambulances were currently pulled up in the breezeway.

Even though it was early on a Friday morning, we had already populated many of the bays in front and several in the back, where more serious trauma cases came. Since Brack was a trauma hospital in an urban center, there were also already different kinds of patients in the bays. Some of these patients were homeless or indigent, others were the working poor who didn't have insurance and had come in for primary health care, usually something that should have been treated days or weeks earlier. Some of the patients were accident victims; one of the patients already in a trauma bay had just been brought in from a motor vehicle accident, and as I watched, fascinated and a little squeamish, the nurses moved in, cut away his bloody pants, stopped the bleeding where his broken femur stuck through the skin. The ER staff moved quickly, expertly, with a minimum of fuss and bother over things that would have most of us screaming. It was simply what they did; they fixed broken bodies supremely well.

Some of the patients had women's issues, although Brackenridge, associated as it was with the Catholic Seton sisters, was not allowed to get into the business of contraceptive health care. One woman had just been wheeled into one of the private examining rooms in the front section reserved for specific kinds of women's medical issues—loss of fetal heartbeat, rape, ectopic pregnancy. When I asked about this woman, her nurse simply told me, "She does *not* want to see a man right now."

I nodded and moved on; I could send a female chaplain later if she expressed a desire to talk to someone.

Some of the patients were incarcerated. On a gurney at the front of the ER, where victims of illness and less serious trauma cases were taken, an inmate—probably from the city jail, although he might also have been from County—lay moaning, his foot naked and purple, some toes broken. His Converse high-top lay forlornly next to that wounded foot; the rest of him, clad in an orange jumpsuit, was handcuffed to the gurney, while a deputy sat nearby, leafing through a magazine.

So, to summarize my initial findings that morning: the poor, the sick, the homeless, the incarcerated. I understood that this early in my experience I was completely out of my depth—I had never, for example, seen my own or anyone else's bones sticking through skin—but I was also, somehow, strangely grateful to be where I was. I don't know what your Jesus looks like, but I thought mine would have felt right at home in the Brackenridge ER. In the Gospels, after all, Jesus typically displays a concern for the suffering, the poor, and those in prison, as in Matthew 25 where he explains what we are supposed to be doing in this world: "For I was hungry and you gave me food, I was thirsty and you gave me something to drink, I was a stranger and you welcomed me, I was naked and you gave me clothing, I was sick and you took care of me, I was in prison and you visited me" (vv. 35–36). Clergy and chaplains may in fact be ridiculous for trying to model themselves after Jesus—he was God, after all, and all of us are mere mortals—but that is the model we've been given, and I thought that in some very real ways, here in this emergency room was where the Christian rubber might meet the road of the world.

When I stepped to the back of the ER where the "crash" bays were located and began talking with the social worker whose office was in a hallway off the main hall, I discovered the first of my patients who had put themselves in the emergency room. In the green-tiled observation bay in the back section of the ER, I saw a pale and sickly woman in her thirties. She was in restraints, her hands tightly bound to the metal rails; she had overdosed the night before. She looked like she had been doing drugs for a good long while, and that summer I would actually see some dead people with more color, which was unfortunate, since she was African American.

I spoke to her from the doorway. We had been instructed to introduce ourselves to the patients, ask if we could be helpful, and not to feel that we were intruding, since hospital staff are in and out of the patient's space at all hours.

But Michelle could not answer, or did not choose to. So I asked the ER social worker if I should check back in on her, attempted suicide being—as I could tell you from my own painful life experience—a sure-fire symptom of spiritual distress.

She looked at me like the ER newbie I was.

"This is not her first time," she said, and she turned her back to me, went back to work. She had a lot to do, and no time or attention to spare for the intentional drug overdose in bay 10.

At first, I was struck by what I thought was coldness in her—in a lot of those working in the ER, in fact. Later I discovered two things. One: like the doctors on "M*A*S*H," people who work in the ER tend to laugh so that they don't cry. They put up walls; many of them feel that they have to. Surrounded by so much suffering on a daily basis, they have to find a coping mechanism or three, ways to shut some of it out, or to defuse it, or bad things will happen to them. And two: I learned that when you work around the clock giving your heart and soul to save lives, people who try to commit suicide just make you mad.

When life is an absolute value, as it is in the ER, then choosing—or attempting to choose—death is like spitting in the faces of those who work there.

Later I would understand that better.

But not that morning.

It was at that moment that the two-way radio on the counter squawked. Always, I would learn, a ravenlike omen of bad news approaching at high speed.

A police car was minutes away, bringing in a pregnant woman in respiratory arrest.

Another drug overdose.

The nurses prepped Crash Bay 4, and when the police hustled this young African American woman into the ER, the hospital staff wheeled her into the bay and started putting her onto life support.

They were too late.

"Code Blue," the announcement went out over the loudspeakers, on every floor in the hospital. "Code Blue."

A code is a hospital emergency; different colors mean different things. Some are more disastrous than Code Blue—they might designate, say, a person with a gun, a combative patient, or a weather emergency—but Code Blue was the one that, as chaplain, I always had to drop whatever I was doing and run to, if it was announced on one of my stations. It meant cessation of life function, someone dead or dying, if the medical staff could not revive them.

And at this moment, this young pregnant woman was dying on the table in front of me.

Nurses and doctors swarmed her, each moving with purpose and expertise. A nurse intubated her—a breathing tube was inserted down her throat, a sign she wasn't capable of breathing on her own—and someone began doing CPR.

From where I stood, I could see that she was very pregnant.

"Goddamn it," one of the ER nurses, Bobby, yelled as they worked on her. Bobby was a nurse in his fifties, and he dressed like a biker, with a bandanna on his head and long grayish-blond hair. Normally he was easygoing, but just now, he was angry. "Damn it all to hell."

Bobby would tell me later that "the mom" had been arrested in a drug raid on her house. Her husband, a drug dealer, was safely in jail. He was fine. But in the back of the squad car, she had tried to hide the evidence. She had swallowed an unknown quantity of crack secreted on her person—later we would discover it was fourteen rocks of crack cocaine—and immediately gone into cardiac arrest.

Now I could not see her for the crowd of people working on her, but I could hear a slow, weak beep, even after the doctor pulled off his mask and sloughed off his gloves, and I knew she was gone. The feeble beep was the sound of the fetal monitor. The mother was dead, but the baby's heart was still beating, at least for a moment.

They took him by caesarean and rushed him into the NICU (neonatal intensive care unit). Not long after, he died too.

She was twenty-four years old.

The baby had been in her womb for twenty-six weeks.

I was still a young chaplain, then, so green that this scene shook me a little bit. It was not my first Code Blue—I'd already been called to three, one of which had been a false alarm. It was not even the first death I witnessed that summer.

But like most Americans, I had been sheltered most of my life from this kind of death and suffering, and this was the first person I saw die in the bloom of life. The fact that it was actually an expectant mother and child made it that much harder to understand. As Stanley Hauerwas has observed, the death of children is particularly jarring to our attempts to make meaning: "The primary task of children is to grow up. . . . Dying children cannot fulfill their fundamental task to have a future."[3]

I thought I had suffered enough myself to develop a stable theological approach to grief and suffering. But still, this experience shook me. It was so horrible. So meaningless.

Where was God in this tragedy?

After they took the baby and covered up the mother, I left the ER, walked back up to the Chaplain's Office on the second floor, and sank into a chair in the corner.

Pablo looked over at me from his computer and asked, "What happened?"

So I told him what I had just seen.

Pablo nodded his head and said, "That's a hard one."

We sat together for a while in silence. Then he asked me, "So what are you thinking?"

What was I thinking?

Well, I did *not* think that God was responsible for this death, and I did *not* believe that God had punished this mother and baby for her sinful ways. *She* had caused this to happen.

But all the same, as I said, when you are confronted with out-of-control tragedy like that—a pregnant mother and her baby!—it brings up all the hard questions.

Where is God in the midst of such suffering?

What is God, that such suffering is permitted?

Who is God, anyway?

They're the same old questions people of faith have always asked. Whenever we face tragedy in the natural world, we look first to explanations, supernatural explanations, if necessary, to explain them. After 9/11, after Hurricane Katrina and the destruction of New Orleans, after the tsunami in the Indian Ocean, after the murders in the Amish school in Pennsylvania or the massacre at Virginia Tech, the call went out: Where was God? What was God doing? Why wasn't God stopping this?

And although there are often perfectly good physical explanations—New Orleans is a coastal city largely built below sea level; weather patterns bring us both pleasant and catastrophic weather; sometimes people get broken inside and do horrible, heinous things—for some reason we want to involve the supernatural in the story. And if we are people of faith, seriously or even nominally, we often want to ask the source of ultimate meaning to help frame some meaning for our own lives.

Our confrontation with God, though, is always going to be shaped by our understanding of God, and that understanding is always going to be personal—and imperfect. In one of the classic definitions of God, Anselm of Canterbury wrote, "O Lord, thou art not only that than which a greater cannot be conceived, but thou art a being greater than can be conceived."[4] If we truly believe that God is God, then any conception that we shape will be necessarily inadequate, limited by our human experience. As the Celtic theologian Philip Newell says, "What can't be said about God is always greater than what can be."

Despite that, most of us have conceptions of God that are static and unchanging. We put God in a box, as the saying goes, delineate God in such a way that life in general and our lives in particular seem to make sense most of the time.

God is an angry deity.
God is a god of peace.
God wants me to be happy.
God will save me if I am faithful.

And we keep God in that box for as long as we can, until something comes along that tears the box open and lets all of the meaning we thought we'd accumulated leak out.

Barbara Brown Taylor has preached about this process of disillusionment and makes clear that it is essential to an authentic spiritual life. If God doesn't come when I call, she says, then that must mean that God is not a collie. If God doesn't fulfill my wishes, then that must mean that God is not a genie. The disillusionment and disappointment we face when we realize we have been wrong about God may be painful, but they do force us to reevaluate our conceptions of God, and if we are honest, to reject our false and inadequate notions of God for a truer one.[5]

So as we continue in this chapter, let's understand that we have to continually wrestle our vision of God into a new box, a new understanding that might better account for evil, suffering, and death—particularly if we believe that God is a God of love, healing, and life.

It's true that no box we can create is big enough. But by recognizing the shape of the box we have created—by owning the stories we have made our own—we can perhaps begin to move toward a new vision, a larger box, a more expansive understanding of God.

And that will give us a greater sense of what we can rightly expect from God when suffering comes.

God as Santa Claus

You know, when I write it like this, in black and white, it looks more than a little ridiculous, doesn't it? And yet, people of faith have often behaved as if God possessed a little black book with the words "naughty" or "nice" inscribed next to their names. If we pray a certain prayer, live in a certain way, perform certain prescribed acts of charity, witness to our faith in Christ, work for social justice, or otherwise comport ourselves in a way that is "nice," then God should rescue us when we find ourselves confronted by distress.

Conversely, if God chooses not to, then this is, for many, a sign that someone is "naughty," even though that naughtiness may be hidden from view. During the years when I suffered from soul-wrenching depression, for example, one of my Christian family members sometimes asked me about secret sin—if there was something I had not acknowledged to God that was hidden from view and might be causing my illness. (And sure, there certainly were things I had kept from the public, but I would think the failure of my marriage, the loss of my son, and my brain full of bad chemicals were probably more to blame than God's disappointment with me.) This naughty/nice story can be insult added to injury when believers are tasked—or blame themselves—for having created the disaster that has broken them or their families. And yet this quid-pro-quo relationship with the Divine is a dominant theology in America even today.

The box-breaking issue for people of faith who believe this transactional story about God, however, emerges when someone who perceives of him- or herself as nice is nonetheless troubled by sickness, loss, or tragedy—things that should only happen to the naughty. I saw this over and over in the hospital, and I think this might be the great crisis of faith for many believers.

It certainly was for Marvella.

Marvella was a sixty-one-year-old African American woman whose presenting symptom was diabetes, which had recently caused her so many health complications that it landed her in the hospital. While she was in the hospital, an opportunistic infection crippled her kidneys. During the summer, I got to know her well, talked with her often, and learned about her life, her family, her sickness, and her faith, which was central to her.

The first time I visited her was on a Sunday early in the summer when I was on call. She had requested that someone bring her a Bible, and after dealing with a string of Code Blues in Brackenridge and other hospitals, I took a Bible from the Chaplain's Office and went up to see her.

Before going in, I talked to her nurse about Marvella's condition, always a good idea, even if I'd looked over medical files; nurses had up-to-the-minute reads of both the medical condition and the patient's state of mind. The nurse told me that Marvella was a lovely and lovable woman who was very sick, that she was growing more and more depressed because she couldn't go home, and that she was unlikely to go home any time soon. That afternoon the doctors had not yet discovered that her kidneys had failed, but they knew something was terribly wrong with her.

When I entered the room and introduced myself, Marvella was watching television, the volume on low. Her curtains were drawn, her room seemed dark and disorderly, and the predominant impression I got was one of sadness, although Marvella greeted me warmly. She used her remote control to raise her bed so that she could look at me as we talked.

I laid the Bible on her table, where she could reach it, and asked how she was feeling.

"Not so good," she said, and I could see it—she looked yellow and drawn. "I'm so tired of being here." Then she held up her hands toward me. "I'm an organist. In church. I just want to get back to doing that for the Lord."

There are several church organists in my family, including my grandmother, who played in her church for fifty years. I felt a great sense of empathy for her, lying here in the hospital. "It must be especially hard to be in here on a Sunday, when you really want to be in church."

She sighed. "Lord, Lord. I play for two choirs. One is the children's choir." Her eyes began to glisten with tears. "I miss those children. Who's going to play for them now?"

She stopped, took a deep breath. "All I want to do is get better so I can go back to doing my work for God. I know God won't leave me here like this. If God has given me this gift, he's not going to leave me here where I can't use it."

She asked me to read her a psalm; her favorite, she said, was Psalm 121:

> I lift up my eyes to the hills—
>   from where will my help come?
> My help comes from the LORD,
>   who made heaven and earth.
>
> He will not let your foot be moved;
>   he who keeps you will not slumber.
> He who keeps Israel
>   will neither slumber nor sleep.
>
> The LORD is your keeper;
>   the LORD is your shade at your right hand.
> The sun shall not strike you by day,
>   nor the moon by night.

The LORD will keep you from all evil;
  he will keep your life.
The LORD will keep
  your going out and your coming in
  from this time on and forevermore.

This is a favorite psalm for the afflicted, and she listened to me read with her eyes half-closed, murmuring "Yes, Lord" here and there.

When I laid the Bible back down, she told me I had just missed her sister, Ora, who had been faithful in visiting her every day. I asked how long she had been in the hospital. Her chart said she had just arrived, but the way she talked made it seem that she had been here much longer.

"I haven't been home since March," she said; it was then the middle of June. "First I was here. Then in that rehabilitation. And now back here. Doesn't seem like I'm ever going to go home."

And then the tears came again. "I thought I was doing right, and that I was living for God. But being here has made me see that I was holding back. I wasn't giving myself to him totally. If I can go home, I'll testify to that. That will be my testimony. I just want to live for God."

Because I was still a newbie, and because her pain touched me, I made a cardinal chaplain's error here—instead of listening to her story and responding in such a way that she could make her own meaning, I felt uncomfortable, and it caused me to say the first stupid thing that came into my head: "Sometimes we have to be knocked off our feet to see something." That's not my theology; although I do believe we learn from adversity, I most certainly do not believe that a loving God intentionally afflicts us so we can learn from it.

But she just sighed. "Lord, Lord. Isn't that the truth."

So we prayed together, and I promised to check back in on her—although she would make an emergency visit to ICU before I saw her again, once they discovered she had suffered a complete renal failure and her other systems were shutting down.

I know God won't leave me here like this.

I thought I was doing right, and that I was living for God. But being here has made me see that I was holding back.

Marvella—like many Christians (and people of other faiths, for that matter)—had a vision of God that was largely contractual. If she did the right things, if she served God faithfully, then God would take care of her. And if not—if she became sick even though she was doing the Lord's work—then there must be something wrong on her end, since, of course, it couldn't be on God's end. Many of our prayers specifically request health, life, God's interaction with our problems; why do we suppose that God might grant such requests?

In the New Testament, we find Jesus telling us that it is appropriate to call upon God and to expect results, as in this passage from the Gospel of Matthew:

> Truly I tell you, whatever you bind on earth will be bound in heaven, and whatever you loose on earth will be loosed in heaven. Again, truly I tell you, if two of you agree on earth about anything you ask, it will be done for you by my Father in heaven. For where two or three are gathered in my name, I am there among them. (Matt. 18:18–20)

Anything you ask, it will be done for you.

But again, what if our Father in heaven doesn't do what we ask? What if we still lose a loved one, suffer illness, get divorced, lose our jobs, even though we have prayed—and lived—faithfully, constantly asking for the exact opposite?

In this story of God as cosmic banker, balancing transactions and divvying out the loot to those who deserve it, the only possible explanation for suffering, if we believe that God is always faithful, is that we have been, somehow, unfaithful and merited our pain. And this also cannot be, for as John Dominic Crossan and Marcus Borg note, God never wills the suffering of the righteous.[6]

Now, I truly doubt that Marvella could amp up her faithfulness and serve God even better; she and her sister Ora were, without doubt, two of the most devout Christians I had ever met. When Marvella decided that she had failed God, I almost wanted to ask how she thought she might serve God more faithfully. Was she going to play for four choirs, maybe sing all seven verses of "Just as I Am" in the moments between rehearsals? But in the story she was living under, God as faithful giver, then she must have done something wrong; otherwise she would be home playing for those children.

God gives to those who are worthy.

Now whatever our philosophies of prayer might be, if we were to stop and think through it, I think few Christians would argue that God owes us anything. Much less would we argue that we have power over God, or that we can induce God to behave in a certain fashion through our actions. We know rationally that what we are talking about in that model is not faith but magic, the use of rites or incantations to cause supernatural powers to grant our wishes. God does not come when we beckon, spread fairy dust when we pray. Yet from the time of God's covenant with the people of Israel up through the Christian understanding of themselves as branches on the tree of Abraham, we have still often had the expectation that God will give us preferential treatment because God likes us best.

Because on God's list of good and bad, there is a "nice" next to our names, and we deserve presents, not coal, when God comes to visit.

For Marvella, who was already a devout woman, strong in her faith, the solution was that she must be stronger yet. If she were living right, God would deliver her, and her promise to do just that if she got well is the kind of magical bargaining I saw often in the hospital, what John Claypool, who learned more than most of us about grief when he lost his young daughter to cancer, called "false promising," an expectation that God's grace to us will come only in a certain shape—the exact thing we asked for.[7]

Frankly, it reminded me of my own bargaining in my childhood Decembers. With a year of not exactly distinguished niceness under my belt, I would write Santa promising I would do better if he would just stop in with the goodies I wanted.

Other outgrowths of this magical mentality may show up in our spiritual practice (if you'll just pray the Prayer of Jabez or whatever may happen to be the popular prayer du jour, then you will be blessed), in stewardship (if you give liberally back to the Lord from what has been given to you, then you will be blessed), and in lifestyle (if you live a moral life, then you will be blessed). But all of these statements contain a structure recognizable to storytellers and computer programmers alike: the if/then statement. If you do one thing, then the other will (must) follow.

And in life, to our great consternation, God sometimes does not seem to recognize the logic of if/then. Marvella and I prayed together for her health; she promised renewed service to God, the Lord she loved and was already serving faithfully.

And she got worse instead of better.

So does this mean we proposed the wrong *if*?

Or does it mean that we imagined the wrong *then*?

The twists and turns of Marvella's story tested my understanding over that summer, and we will speak of them again. But for now, let me say that I recognized a familiar understanding of God that was unraveling before my eyes, a contractual understanding that had been the basis of much of her faith and spiritual practice. And while it was not my particular story of God, helping Marvella come to some provisional acceptance of her sickness required that I empathize with her and begin to imagine with her how God might be working in the world even if I could not understand the mechanisms.

My Grandma Irene, a longtime member of the Assembly of God, believes fervently in the power of committed prayer, and that God answers every prayer. But she also believes that God answers prayer in three ways: yes, no, and wait.

Clearly Marvella's prayer was not being answered with a "yes."

Which left "no" or "wait," and neither of those answers made any sense to her under the terms of the contract she imagined. If God was active in the world, where was he? Why wasn't he giving her what she deserved?

God as Cosmic Champion

Candy was another woman I met in Brackenridge who was asking that question. I first encountered her on my list of Brackenridge patients who, according to the computer system, had requested a chaplain visit; every morning the system had such a list for me, although the patients often had no recollection of asking for a chaplain. After checking over the medical charts of several patients that I would visit on my first trip of the day, I went up to the eighth floor.

I saw through Candy's door that she was out of bed, and when I knocked and entered, noticed that she was simultaneously holding the various tubes and things she was attached to and trying to plug something into the electric outlet behind her. The room was well lit, her curtains open to the Austin skyline. The TV was tuned to a game show, the volume up high. It was a room full of distractions.

Candy herself was fortyish, attractive in a hard sort of way. She had makeup on—a little unusual for patients in the hospital—and her blonde hair was pulled back into a ponytail.

I walked to the end of her bed, introduced myself, and said, "I came by to see how you're feeling this morning."

She looked up at me, a little suspicious, as she continued to probe at the wall with the plug. "Did that lady chaplain tell you about me? I had my operation yesterday, you know."

Nobody had told me anything, but it was good to know someone else had seen her; that also explained why the computers had thought she needed a chaplain in the first place—she was having an operation.

After plugging whatever it was into the wall, she motioned for me to sit in the chair by her left side and rearranged herself back up on the bed, pulling the sheet up over herself. We made small talk: She told me that a friend had come by to do her makeup, talked a little about the operation, and told me that she was on morphine for the pain. Then she asked me, "You know what endometriosis is?"

"I know a little bit about it," I said, danger signals going off in my male head. I knew that men don't get it, that it was one of those female below-the-waist conditions, and that it was reputed to hurt like hell.

"They had to do a hysterectomy yesterday. I've had all kinds of problems down there over the years." She paused for a second and, with no particular emphasis, as though she were talking about someone besides herself, said, "There's a history of abuse."

Her eyes flashed across to see how I was going to take that, but I just looked at her steadily and told her that I was sorry. "No one should have to experience that."

"When I was thirteen months old, my uncle started molesting me," she went on. Her eyes were dry, but I could hear the anger in her voice. "Full penetration. He tore me up inside. I've had so many things wrong with me. He hurt me so bad. You can't do that to a baby."

She looked at me again, held me in her gaze now as if she were testing me. "Does it bother you to hear about this?"

"Of course it does," I said. "But that's why I'm here. I want to know about your life, what you're thinking about."

Then she pulled back the blanket and raised her gown a bit to show me a scar running the length of her thigh; she had tried to cover it with some kind of tattoo, but the scar was still visible beneath. When she was very young and had tried to tell someone about the sexual abuse, she said, her uncle had slashed her leg with a knife, and her mother had locked her down in the basement, her cut bound with duct tape. They didn't let her out again until they thought she had learned her lesson. She had sat in her own blood and filth for days.

Candy looked across at me again, a tremor in her voice as she went on. "That wasn't right, you know? I used to ask why God let that happen to me. Where was God when he was doing that to me? I was mad. With God." She bit her lip, got herself back under control. She wasn't going to cry, no matter what. "I mean, I was just a kid, right? Who was looking out for me?"

Her life had been a mess. She had been in and out of prison. But one day, while participating in a prison ministry, she had finally come to a point of clarity.

"I forgave them for hurting me. My family. They was full of the devil." She nodded emphatically and went on. "The devil made them act like that. They took drugs and drank too much. It's not an excuse. But it was part of why they did them things."

This is not my particular theology of evil, but it is one I heard a lot in hospitals that summer, and had heard since my childhood in the evangelical traditions in which I was raised.

I used to ask why God let that happen to me.

They was full of the devil.

One of the most prominent stories about God is that God is a partner in a dualistic dance of good and evil. Many American Christians believe that God and the diabolical figure we call Satan are locked in a no-holds-barred struggle for the future of existence. Their understanding of suffering and death is that they are intimately connected to sin and Satan: the first set exists because of the second. While the apostle Paul tells us in Romans 6 that Jesus' resurrection has provided the ultimate victory over sin and death, this idea of potent personified evil is hard to discard, and it does make a certain amount of sense in explaining the continuing presence of death and suffering in a universe created by a benevolent God.

It also causes a theological problem for us, though: this dualistic way of thinking elevates Satan from simply being the Adversary who serves God, Satan's role in the Hebrew Bible in the book of Job, for example, to the role of a competing deity who has either been given or seized control of the world. Because of humankind's fall into sin, Satan thus is assumed to have power over human beings, power not only to tempt, but also perhaps even actual power to compel, to control, to contend.[8]

Now, of course, you may not believe in a Prince of Darkness who struggles with the God of Light for the fate of humanity or of individual human souls. As Walter Wink points out in *Unmasking the Powers*, the best way to stop all conversation in certain company is to mention your belief in angels, spirits, or Satan, and nonbelievers as well as certain people of faith may have this same reaction.[9]

But as my patient Candy demonstrates, many people still believe that God is supposed to be our champion in the cosmic battle between good and evil. As Candy understood her story, God could have intervened against the power of evil; God should have. So when sin, suffering, and destruction prevail, as they did in her case, then something seems to be very wrong in the universe.

This is the classic problem of what theologians call *theodicy*: Why do death and evil exist in our universe if God is good? It is, of course, possible to build a story of God that simply says God is God and I am not, so who am I to ask questions about how God chooses to conduct this cosmic struggle? That sort of acceptance is one of the interpretations, as we will see in chapter 3, of the book of Job, and it certainly exists in sentiments like that of Paul in the Christian Testament—"For now we see in a mirror, dimly, but then we will see face to face. Now I know only in part; then I will know fully, even as I have been fully known" (1 Cor. 13:12)—or as in the old gospel song: "We'll understand it/All by and by."

Augustine, in *The City of God*, delivered a classic theological understanding of God's action—or inaction—in the life of the world by arguing that God does indeed have an absolute and perfect interest in justice, but that it is unknowable to us as humans until the coming of the Parousia—until, that is, God perfects all things. We must simply trust that whether or not we understand it, "that which is hidden is just."[10] If we will only wait and see, we will discover that everything God has done has been in the service of justice and life against the forces of evil and death.

But it still can be hard for us to accept this—hard for Job, hard for Candy, hard for you and me—because we long to understand in the here and now. That's why it may be helpful for us to examine the shape of this story of cosmic struggle. As I said in the introduction, understanding more about the stories we have accepted as our own can often lead us to recognitions about where and how they fall short or fail to explain everything for us, and I think that this is one of those places.

We can trace this opposition of supernatural forces of good and evil all the way back to several lines of ancient and non-Christian thought, a genealogy that might surprise many Christians whose faith embraces the existence of Satan, and who consciously or unconsciously have granted Satan power to contend with God. Both the pre-Christian religion of Zoroastrianism and the third-century faith of the Manicheans postulated a dualistic system in which a god of good and a god of evil strove for supremacy. In Zoroastrianism, the good god, Ahura Mazda, was in contention with an evil god,

Angra Mainyu, or Ahriman; the faith's founder, Zoroaster (also known as Zarathustra), called his followers to be aware of this cosmic dichotomy and to make their own choices accordingly.

This dualistic vision of gods in conflict was influential across the ancient world. Louis Jacobs (among others) suggests that the character of Satan might have developed from Zoroastrianism, and that prophets such as Isaiah (or Second Isaiah, as this writer is sometimes more particularly identified) spoke out against the pervasiveness and perversity of this understanding of the cosmic order, as here in Isaiah:

> I am the LORD, and there is no other;
>   besides me there is no god.
>   I arm you, though you do not know me,
> so that they may know, from the rising of the sun
>   and from the west, that there is no one besides me;
>   I am the LORD, and there is no other.
> I form light and create darkness,
>   I make weal and create woe;
>   I the LORD do all these things.[11]

For Candy and people with a similar understanding of God—including many people in my own family—God has power to shield the helpless and the faithful from the supernatural power of darkness, which is tangible and present. When loss and suffering assail us, it simply represents another bout in the cosmic contest, another opportunity for God to win by a knockout. Even though, if you put the question to them directly, they would doubtless deny that Satan is anywhere nearly as powerful as God, the fact that some believers put Satan in the ring against God at all suggests a certain parity.

The problem of pain for this story, simply put, has to do with God's failure to leave the dressing room. If God does not save—or cannot save—then what does this say about God? It is here that many faith systems break down, particularly when a person of faith believes that God has a certain responsibility to act. In Candy's case, the impetus was clear: She was only a child, powerless to protect herself. God should have watched over her, as in all those childhood prayers.

Why didn't God do that?

For others, the responsibility strikes them less as a cosmic conflict, and more as a formal and binding covenant: God is obligated to act on behalf of people of faith because of a contract, express or implied. Many Christians believe—consciously or subconsciously—that if a person of faith acts in the correct fashion, then God has a corresponding obligation to act.

God as Parent

My grandma's statement about prayer and God's possible answers takes on embodied life around my house, where I myself am the somewhat powerful entity being asked for things by my ten-year-old son Chandler. When he asks for these things, sometimes I say yes. Sometimes I say no. Sometimes I say "We'll see" (which actually means no, as I think Chandler has begun to notice).

This similarity between the role of the parent and the perceived role of God in our lives leads many of us to imagine a relationship between us and God that works in the same sort of way. As Jouette Bassler has observed, "the God who demands and who will judge is also the Father who can be appealed to in prayer with familiar intimacy."[12] So the story of God as parent and us as God's children is a story we must examine in order to discover the expectations it might create for us when trouble strikes.

One of my most difficult on-call nights began with a call to Seton Northwest. The nurse told me it was for a fetal demise, and not just any fetal demise: the mother had just given birth to twins; the first had died in her womb weeks ago, but they had lost the second just hours ago.

The father and mother were Ethiopian Christians, and they were in the birthing room together, quietly grieving when I arrived. They were waiting for her mother and sisters. I felt that when the family showed up, then things would really begin, that the grief they were holding in politely as they spoke with me would surface and be shared among them.

But we talked, and quietly, the parents affirmed their faith in the midst of their pain. The mother said, "I believe my babies are with God."

And then they asked me if I would find and baptize their babies, and I told them that if it was important to them, of course I would baptize them.

After I left them, the nurse took me back to a storeroom behind the nurse's station. There, she brought me the tiny bodies of the boys in plastic canisters—the kind I might use to store cereal or lentils on top of my refrigerator. One, the twin who had been dead for weeks, was gray, wrinkled, half the size of his brother. The boy who had just died was still pink and looked almost alive.

I opened my Book of Common Prayer, turned back to the section on baptism, and, then, gently, sprinkled holy water on each of them in turn and said, "I baptize you in the name of the Father, and of the Son, and of the Holy Spirit."

Although baptism is a holy sacrament, my tradition teaches that a layperson can perform an emergency baptism when time is of the essence. In this case, it was important to these parents that their babies be baptized, even in death. It symbolized something to them that would make it easier to accept that their boys were truly in the hands of God.

For the apostle Paul, baptism into the faith of Jesus Christ resurrected was an adoption into the family of God. In Galatians 4 and Romans 8, he wrote about the difference between who we were before, our identity before we came to follow Jesus, and who we were after, beloved adopted children of a gracious Father.

This story in which God is like a parent to us is reinforced by many passages in the Bible, of course. The metaphor of God as stern or loving father is a primary way we experience God in Scripture; one of the main images of God in the Hebrew Bible, according to John Scullion, is that of the one who creates and blesses.[13] In the Psalms, God is a "father of the fatherless" (68:5 KJV), and we are assured that "As a father has compassion for his children, so the LORD has compassion for those who fear him" (103:13). In Proverbs, we read:

My child, do not despise the LORD's discipline
or be weary of his reproof,
for the LORD reproves the one he loves,
as a father the son in whom he delights.

(3:11–12)

Throughout the Christian Testament, we are also given the image of God as Father. Jesus, of course, continually refers to God as Father, even, affectionately, as Abba (daddy or papa), but we are encouraged to acknowledge God as our own father as well. The Lord's Prayer, the model for prayer given to his followers by Jesus, is directed to "Our Father," after all.

For this reason, it's not surprising to recognize, along with Rabbi Harold Kushner, that one of the stories that most of us tell about God is that God is a father (or, beautifully, in Luke 13, a mother hen) who watches over us, protects us, corrects us, and loves us. As Rabbi Kushner wrote, God for many of us is a parent like our earthly parents, only better:

> If we were obedient and deserving, He would reward us. If we got out of line, he would discipline us, reluctantly but firmly. He would protect us from being hurt or from hurting ourselves, and would see to it that we got what we deserved in life.[14]

Except, of course, as we are already seeing, this correlation we imagine between our behavior and God's behavior doesn't seem to hold true. If Chandler takes advantage of his big brother Jake's forbearance and smacks him, I will make sure there are immediate and negative consequences. But in life, when we do something wrong, even something terrible, we know that there isn't always an immediate consequence, and some people never seem to be punished for the bad they do. What kind of parent is God if God allows people to get away with doing what any good human parent would punish?

Conversely, as in Marvella's case (and with most of the other figures you will meet in these pages), the punishment people sometimes seem to be receiving from God is out of all proportion to any offense they may have committed. Does my cheating on my taxes—or on my spouse—require that my innocent daughter should be hit by a car? Of course not! No good earthly parent would ever assign this sort of unjust punishment. So why would we imagine that a just and loving God would work that way?

Here again we find a story that is straining against the sides of its box. The image of God as parent is a powerful devotional tool, and suggests an earthly analogue for the deity whose love and care for us brought us into being and preserves us. But clearly this story doesn't hold together when unearned tragedy strikes, or unpunished evil continues. How can we reconcile our desire for God to be actively involved in our lives and yet accept that our relationship is not precisely that of parent to child?

Let's keep looking.

God alongside Us

Pamela was a thirty-seven-year-old Anglo woman who had terminal brain cancer, and although her nurses and doctors were of course sympathetic to her situation, she was also driving them crazy. Her night nurse called me at four o'clock one morning and urged me to come up and talk to her, saying, "She needs something."

Clearly what she meant was, "She needs something more than I can give her." As I rolled out of bed, yawning and tired, the nurse told me that Pamela hadn't slept for days, that she was asking the nurses for ever bigger doses of sleep meds and for pain pills several times an hour, and biggest problem of all, she was resisting the clear suggestion of her medical staff that there was nothing more they could do for her in the hospital (a secular faith story about which I will have more to say in chap. 2).

I arrived outside Pamela's room about 4:30 a.m. and found her nurse, who looked as exhausted as I felt. She told me that Pamela's cancer was untreatable, and that she was much more likely to get sick there on the ward from staph or some other opportunistic infection than to get better from any medical intervention they could perform for her at this point.

"So I hope you can talk her into going home," she said, and then she pushed me into the room with obvious relief.

Pamela and I had a long visit, and there were a lot of issues haunting her, both physical and spiritual. She was filled with grief at the thought of leaving her teenaged son behind. She was worried about how her husband, who was "a baby in the faith," would deal with her death. She was scared about that death, and because she was a devout Christian, she was trying to make sense of God's purpose at the same time as she was asking me to pray hard for divine intervention. She talked for over an hour, and as I got up to go, I promised to come back again.

On our second visit, after she had brought me up to date on her last visit with the doctors, who still wanted to discharge her, I asked Pamela a question: "Do you think God understands your pain?"

A sad smile spread across her face. "I know he does. Jesus died on the cross for the worst of sinners. He experienced pain and death. God knows pain, and he knows my pain. He sees everything."

"Do you believe that God is walking beside you in your pain?"

She considered for a moment, took a deep breath. "I believe it. But sometimes I forget. I get scared. Right now it's here with me— I can feel him. But when it's late, or when I'm scared and hurting, I can't always keep that feeling."

On a surprisingly dramatic episode from the first season of the medical situation comedy *Scrubs*, one of the young doctors, Turk (Donald Faison), a devout Christian, pulls duty in the ER on Christmas Eve, and it turns out to be a disastrous evening that fills him with serious doubts about God. When his girlfriend, Carla (Judy Reyes), tells him to calm down, he says,

> **Turk:** Baby, you don't know how I feel!
>
> **Carla:** Well, then, tell me!
>
> **Turk:** I feel abandoned! All my life, I believed that God listens to our prayers, and that he cares for us, and that he watches over us. And last night, there were so many people that needed to be watched over. How am I supposed to believe in someone that

> is willing to let innocent people suffer? Huh? Answer me.
> Please!
>
> **Carla:** I can't.[15]

We've seen how transactional thinking, the vision of God as cosmic champion, and the notion that God is a loving and correcting parent inform many of our God-stories, and thus our notions about where God is (or should be) in our grief. The power of magical thinking exemplified by our prayers for supernatural intervention comes from our conception that although God may have established the natural order, God can also intervene in that order whenever it is called for—as in the need to stop the suffering of innocent people.

We need to think a little bit about the theology of divine intervention. Thomas Aquinas concluded that God was unchanging and immutable—and the God in our box, whatever he, she, or it looks like, may also have the virtue of being eternal and static. But Aquinas found an out; like Augustine, earlier, he argued that God could miraculously intervene in human affairs because this possibility of intervention was part of the natural order of creation as well.[16]

The miracles we pray for are thus a part of this "ultimate order and plan of creation," and so we need not imagine that they are outside the scope of God or God's created universe.[17] Divine interventions could be possible, because, simply put, the classical notion is that God can do what God wants to do.

But this miraculous God is not the only story of God that people of faith have told over the years, and it's not necessarily the healthiest one. (Rabbi Kushner points out that many of our God-stories imagine that God has caused our pain—or at the very least, failed to end it, since the Almighty could choose to do so.)[18] Celtic Christianity, however, suggests another way of understanding God and God's place in suffering. It begins from a position that doesn't postulate a God removed from creation who happens to step in from time to time to save the innocent, cure cancer, or find someone's garage door opener. In the Celtic tradition, God the creator isn't distant, but present, and God the Son is often considered to be a holy companion walking alongside us on every journey, since he knows every element of human life and death. In the words of an ancient Irish prayer, "The Litany of Creation": "The path I walk, Christ walks it." Many of the ancient Celtic prayers, including the famous "lorica" (also called "St. Patrick's Breastplate"), thus invoke Christ's presence and protection, and in fact, the Celts saw all three persons of the Trinity as immanent. It is a vision of God sharply at odds with notions of separation between heaven and earth, between the physical world and the spiritual one.

In addition to God's nearness, the early Irish, Welsh, and Scottish Christians saw themselves as being surrounded by angels and saints, by all the great cloud of witnesses described in Hebrews 12, not removed into another distant realm but close enough to touch. As Irish priest John J. Ó Ríordáin writes, "the living and the dead are not separated from each other by time and space. As far as the Celts are concerned, the otherworld and this world overlap and interpenetrate."[19] Whether or not your theology comfortably encompasses such figures as angels and saints, the Celtic idea of heaven being "a foot and a half above a man's head" should bring comfort that God does not abandon us and is in fact always in close proximity.

In the Celtic tradition, God not only accompanies us throughout life but is also present at the moment of death. A beautiful death hymn from the Scottish Western Isles reads,

> The shade of death lies upon thy face, beloved,
> But the Jesus of Grace has His hand round about thee;
> In nearness to the Trinity farewell to thy pains,
> Christ stands before thee and peace is in His mind.[20]

In the Celtic tradition, God walks alongside us in life and stands beside us at death, prepared to help us make the short journey from one place to the next, from where we are now back to where we began. Death becomes not a pawn in a cosmic chess match of good and evil and not a punishment for broken promises or bad behavior, but a natural part of the created world to which God is so closely linked, a part of the created order. God's role in such an understanding is not to halt death and suffering, but to abide with those who suffer, first in this realm, and then in the next.

Death to the Celts remains painful and mysterious, but in this understanding (and in others), it is also beautiful, for it reunites us with the God who loves us, and if we can face this, perhaps it will make all the difference in how we face grief and suffering. Philip Newell writes that "to name the reality of death for ourselves, and to believe that in it is a grace that can be responded to, is to be liberated, whether we live or whether we die."[21] In other words, death is not a disaster, but an opportunity; an opportunity to return home to ultimate connection with the God who created us.

God as Coworker in Creation

And if this hope of ultimate connection might be true of death, could it also be true in life?

For some years in the late 1990s and early 2000s I was desperately sick with chronic depression. One night in October of 2001 I staggered home to my dark apartment in Austin after drunkenly disgracing myself in front of my ex-wife and my son Chandler at her birthday party. I had agreed to go to the party to supervise Chandler, who wanted to celebrate his mom's birthday, but I couldn't bear the thought of meeting the man she was dating or of being around a large group of strangers—couldn't imagine doing it sober, at least. And so I had gone to the party well into my second six-pack of Corona, and before the night was over, I had gotten into a horrible, screaming fight with her in front of God and Chandler and everyone.

When I got home from ruining her birthday party, I was sick unto death—sick in my very soul. During the years that I had suffered from serious depression, I had several times come up to the very threshold of suicide, and that night, as I considered the pain I had caused, the pain I was in, and the grief I felt over the loss of my marriage and my daily life with my son, the only solution that seemed to make sense was to kill myself.

I had a nearly full bottle of sleeping pills in my medicine cabinet, left over after my unhappy realization a year before that I had become addicted to them. When the image of that almost-full bottle of pills flashed into my mind, it was decided. I began to shake, and tears began to come, because I knew in that moment that unless something stopped me, I was going to take them all, and in the morning I would be dead.

Something did indeed intervene, although it was not God interposing some enormous divine hand between me and my bathroom cabinet. Not directly, at least.

But as I was rocking back and forth on my haunches on the floor of my apartment, weeping uncontrollably, my hand happened to brush against my cell phone, which had fallen under the couch.

I picked it up, and on an impulse, I called my friend Chris Seay, although he rarely answers his phone, and certainly not this far past his bedtime. But then I heard his voice saying, "Hey, Buddy, what's up?" and before I knew it, I was telling him everything that had happened and what I was afraid I was about to do.

And he listened, and told me it was OK to feel bad, but that he loved me, still, and he was pretty sure God did too.

During the times that I was sickest from depression—when death seemed like a welcome thing, less frightening and certainly less painful than going on living and hurting—I prayed hard for healing, I bargained and negotiated, and I may in fact have had prayers answered. But what proved to be a vital element of my recovery was the physical companionship of Christians who were willing to be coworkers with God in helping to put the world right—or at least, to labor in my suffering corner of it.

My friends Chris, Tom, and Scott, my priest Greg Rickel (now Bishop Rickel of Olympia), and a handful of others who loved me, lived out the Celtic idea of holy companionship in the midst of my suffering. They never suggested to me that God was going to take my suffering away, and they didn't suggest that if I changed my life or my behavior, God would like me better. They simply walked alongside me, a tangible reminder that I was loved, valued, a child of God worth saving.

And then one day I looked up to discover that I was well, whole, and capable of walking alongside others in their distress.

The notion of God as a deity in process is a vision of God worth our consideration, even though it represents a stark contrast to the immutable and unfeeling God of Aquinas, Augustine, and Anselm. It is a God-story with contemporary relevance, and it may be liberating for those of us who wrestle with the question "Why did God allow this to happen?" by proposing that perhaps God cannot—or does not—intervene in such affairs. Rowan Williams, Archbishop of Canterbury, suggested after the September 11 terrorist attacks that the world is ordered in such a fashion that evil and suffering can't simply be thwarted by God's impulse to do so: "Where would he stop, for goodness sake? He'd have to be intervening every instant of human history."[22] And David Ray Griffin imagines that while God might be active in human history, that action may not come in the form of supernatural intervention, as we've always imagined. He suggests that "God constantly works to overcome the evil in the creation with good, and in human experience he does this by simultaneously seeking to increase our enjoyment of life and to enlist our support."[23] In this story, God moves to change the world not by miraculous intervention that moves us around like pieces on a playing field, but by encouragement and sympathetic love, by being a God we choose to work alongside.

Giving up the notion of God as a cosmic superhero does in some ways clank against the classical conceptions of God as all-powerful, all-knowing, and all-good. It may be less soothing than the notion that an omnipotent ally has a safety net in place below us. But this story does seem to make a certain kind of sense in a world where calamitous evil like the Holocaust, the development and use of the atomic bomb, and soul-rending disasters like 9/11 and the South Pacific tsunami test our notion of a perfect, settled, and loving God.

Process theology is drawn from the early-twentieth-century teaching and writing of the English mathematician and philosopher Alfred North Whitehead, who suggested that God's essence was not that of Unmoved Mover, as Aristotle proposed, or of essential being, as Aquinas had argued. In this vision of God, as Rowan Williams notes, grief and suffering "have to be confronted, suffered, taken forward, healed in the complex process of human history, always in collaboration with what we do and say and pray."[24] So where is God in this process of human history? Well, in a sense, God (not the devil!) is in the details: Many process theologians argue that "this entire cosmic process is God, and God works like an artist attempting to win order and beauty out of opportunity."[25]

The idea of God as process—or even in process—does differ dramatically from traditional stories of God (our notion of omnipotence, certainly, or of God using his power to order creation to his whim goes out the window), but it offers other consolations.[26] For one, it offers the idea of a God capable of suffering alongside us, and not just in the experience of Jesus Christ, who knew suffering and death as we do. In the classical view of God shaped by theologians like Augustine, Anselm, and Aquinas, God was perfect and unchanging. If God is intransitory, then God can't possibly experience powerful emotion, which comes and goes. As Aquinas noted, God's wrath is not like human wrath, since "anger and the like are [only] attributed to God on account of a similitude of effect."[27] So how can we feel that our creator understands us if God does not experience transformative emotions like anger, sadness, and joy, as we do?

Some contemporary theologians have argued that suffering humanity actually needs a suffering God. Jürgen Moltmann, for example, suggests that in the crucifixion of Christ, the entire Trinity actually experienced pain, that the cross of Christ was also "God's death and God's suffering."[28] In this story, God becomes one who knows our pain by being one who is capable of feeling pain, not merely the similitude of it.

A process-related story of God also offers us the opportunity to be coworkers with God to create the world we wish to see. If God is life, truth, and love, then God's impulse must always be toward healing, toward wholeness, toward justice, and we are permitted to align ourselves with God in this goal of building the kingdom. As Rowan Williams noted above, what we do and say and pray is our collaboration in the divine purpose and process. Archbishop Desmond Tutu goes a step further when he argues that the faithful "are the agents of transformation that God uses to transfigure His world."[29]

In this vision, God does not magically eliminate suffering, but, as Tutu notes, "he bears it with us and strengthens us to bear it."[30] To know that our suffering is shared both by God and by those doing the work of God may be a powerful recompense to our loss of the notion that God will or can eliminate evil and death. It can also be a powerful impetus to us to live so that we truly act like partners in this cosmic work of hope.

The stories we have examined in this chapter represent some of the most prominent beliefs that contemporary believers hold about God and God's place in the universe. One or more of them may offer something appealing for you. But ultimately, you will need to piece together your own understanding of God so that you can make sense for yourself of where God is—or is supposed to be—in relation to suffering.

Remember that any conception we create, however well thought out or faithfully followed, is still just a box in which we carry our understanding of God. So if you believe that God will wipe away every tear and yet you're still crying, then maybe your box is broken—not your faith. If you believe God will heal your mother if you only pray hard enough, and yet she still suffers— then perhaps your box is broken, not your prayer life. And above all, we have to remember that if God exists, then he/she/it/they is (are?) ultimately unknowable, above and outside the biggest boxes we can even imagine.

But isn't that why we require faith? If we understood everything about God, then what reason would we have to exercise belief?

But, faith is a challenge to us, particularly in the face of loss. As Søren Kierkegaard wrote in *Fear and Trembling*, the movement to faith is irrational. It requires first a resignation and renunciation of will like that of Abraham in the face of his son Isaac's death, a resignation so extreme that Kierkegaard's narrator announces that ultimately there is nothing he can learn from Abraham except to be astonished by him.[31] And resignation may be as far as some are able to get. One of my seminary students, Eric Hungerford, wrote in a paper about *Fear and Trembling*, "People who mistake their naïve optimism for faith stop at the point of resignation, thinking that they have lost faith." It is here, actually, that faith becomes supremely necessary. Our relationship to God should not be merely one of naive optimism; as we have said (and will say again), it should be about authentic and tenacious hope, even in the presence of death and despair.

Faith is a challenging thing. Although we know what faith is—the author of Hebrews writes that "faith is the assurance of things hoped for, the conviction of things not seen. . . . By faith we understand that the worlds were prepared by the word of God, so that what is seen was made from things that are not visible" (11:1, 3)—we nonetheless have a hard time holding onto belief in the invisible. I mean, we have a hard enough time understanding forces we can see at work, as we will discover in our next chapter. But it's worth cultivating that conviction that allows us to believe some things absolutely and fearlessly, even if we can never perfectly understand them; it is, in fact, a necessary thing.

And how much easier that belief is, once you find a story worth believing.

Chapter Two

"I Don't Deserve This"

Stories of Grief and Modern American Myth

We Americans are the peculiar, chosen people . . . God has predestinated, mankind expects, great things from our race; and great things we feel in our souls.

Herman Melville, *White-Jacket*

American Myths

As we learned in the previous chapters, we use stories to make sense of our lives, and our awareness and understanding of those stories matters; as philosopher Alisdair McIntyre writes, "I can only answer the question 'What am I to do?' if I can answer the prior question 'Of what story or stories do I find myself a part?'"[1]

Unfortunately, often we are not consciously aware of the cultural stories in which we may have found ourselves swimming. Many of the most potent and powerful stories—these "master narratives" that surround us and shape us—are those we have grown up believing just because we are alive and sentient in the United States of America in the twenty-first century, not because we've thoughtfully chosen them for ourselves.

These modern American master narratives—we might also call them American *myths*, if by myth we mean a larger-than-life story that helps us to orient ourselves and to create meaning—are so pervasive that we may not even recognize that we have adopted them as our own and are living our lives by them. Some of them might even be counter to our expressed values. But they have incredible power over us nevertheless. In our exploration of stories of suffering, we must also consider these American master narratives from the outset, since they shape so many of our responses to grief. Once we have identified them and become sensitized to our complicity in accepting them, then we can begin to evolve our own stories, shaped by choice and not simply by cultural immersion.

By and large, these American myths rotate around the generic modern Western notion of progress, the idea that through self-examination, discovery, and knowledge, humankind will gradually become peaceful, fulfilled, and happy. N.T. Wright suggests that modern faith in "automatic progress" has grown out of the secular narratives of "technological achievement, medical advancement, Romantic pantheism, Hegelian progressive Idealism and social Darwinism," concepts that created the climate both private and public in which most people in the West lived—and continue to live—out their lives.[2] These general progress myths of the modern West have been supplemented here by Yankee pragmatism, American can-do-ism, absolute faith in capitalism, under-recognized trust in neo-imperialism—and a liberal sprinkling of Hollywood endings and Disney pixie dust.

The end result, as we will see, is a culture in which suggesting anything other than that boundless progress is not only possible but probable is to be branded "pessimistic." As Dan P. McAdams writes in *The Redemptive Self: Stories Americans Live By*, an American narrative that doesn't suggest the possibility of success, healing, emancipation, and enlightenment is disastrous in the eyes of the culture, it being "un-American to take issue with the redemptive self," since American narratives are so strongly tied up in the myth of continuing upward mobility, success, and wholeness.[3]

And to actually fail at something in our culture—whether that failure is divorce, illness, or death—is simply to *be* a failure. Many of us honestly seem to believe that with the proper nutrition, counseling, exercise regimen, or eye shadow, virtually every problem in life can be solved, or at least held at bay until science has created—or someone is selling—a solution. Things need never end badly in America; there are always solutions for the prepared, the thinkers, the believers.

Only failures need to suffer.

So to be an American in the early twenty-first century is to believe that not only do we live in the greatest nation in the history of the world, but that this identity will shield us from grief and suffering—if only we act with preemptive resolve and wisdom.

In this chapter's epigraph, we discovered that wise old Yankee novelist Herman Melville saying in the nineteeth century what Henri Nouwen argued in more contemporary times: that Americans accept it as an article of faith that life will always meet their needs.[4] We Americans have actually enshrined our desire for and belief in happiness not just in our narratives, but even in our formative documents. How many other nations believe their citizens have an absolute right to "life, liberty, and the pursuit of happiness"?

H. Richard Niebuhr defined faith as "the dependence of a living self on centers of value whence it derives its worth and for the sake of which it lives."[5] If we accept this definition, which seems like a pretty good one to me, it becomes apparent that many Americans have expanded the notion of faith to the extent that many of us fervently believe in happy endings and soft landings, technology and medicine, free markets and the power of consumerism, or the beauty of American civilization as much as—or more than—we believe in the God of Abraham and Sarah, of Isaac and Rebekah, of Jacob, Leah, and Rachel. If this is true, then even those of us who call ourselves people of faith may have chosen to live stories that are more about faith in country, faith in commerce, or faith in science than they are about the "radical monotheism" or absolute and only faith in the true God that Niebuhr argued was the greatest story we could ever know.[6]

We've already seen that the vast majority of Americans say that we believe in God.

It's just all the other things in which we believe that may ultimately cause us so much consternation.

The God of Happiness

It simplifies history a bit too much, maybe, but I still blame Benjamin Franklin for the supremely pragmatic can-do spirit of Americans, who certainly can boast a great history of solved problems. In the opening pages of his *Autobiography*, Franklin gives his ostensible reason for writing:

> Having emerged from the Poverty and Obscurity in which I was born and bred, to a State of Affluence and some Degree of Reputation in the World, and having gone so far through life with a considerable Share of Felicity, the conducing Means I made use of, which with the Blessing of God so well succeeded, my Posterity may like to know, as they may find some of them suitable to their own Situations, and therefore fit to be imitated.[7]

The image of Franklin in his autobiography that has been such an influence on American thought is that of a young man who goes from rags to riches through hard work, who resolves to chart his way to perfection, eliminating one "errata" (not sin; *never* sin) at a time, and who becomes a model citizen through his civic service and his success in business. In later life, Franklin may have been balding, bulging, and suffering from bad eyesight, but today, Americans can fix even these problems. In any case, Franklin was optimistic enough to create a narrative template and suggest that stories such as his were actually the story of American life, that all Americans, imitating Franklin, might expect (at the very least) a considerable share of felicity.

Swept up in this myth, Americans believe that given some forethought and tenacity, all potential problems can be swept away—an admirable but ultimately wrong-headed reading of reality. And caught up in the complementary myth of happiness, we have come to believe that not only *can* we sweep away these problems, but that we *deserve* their complete disappearance into the dustbin. Grief and suffering, as we saw in chapter 1, are not supposed to bother us if we only do the right things, and if you think this belief seems like a form of secular magical thinking rather than a spiritual kind, then you may have noted the only real difference between them.

You have met Marvella, the devoutly Christian organist with the failing kidneys, and I suggested to you that she wrestled increasingly hard to understand her continually sinking health. At first she was unfailingly optimistic, sure that her doctors and her God were not only on her side, but actively solving every health problem to her satisfaction.

She was doing the right things, she was a good person, and she deserved to get well.

Later, largely at the impetus of her even more devout sister, Ora, Marvella began to suspect the action of Satan against her. He could afflict her body; he could attack her spirit. But if the Prince of Darkness thought he could keep her down, he had another think coming. God would see her distress and her faithfulness and rescue her.

Then later, as she learned that her kidneys had failed and that she would have to undergo dialysis, perhaps every week for the rest of her life, she lost her nerve and maybe—for a tiny bit—her faith. Where before, she had pushed herself painfully upright to talk about God when I knocked on her door, she now lay listlessly—one might even say hopelessly—when I tried to speak with her.

It was as if suddenly the talk of God bored her. It was as if we were talking about an old boyfriend who had begun well, but who had ultimately disappointed her.

"I've done everything I was supposed to do, Greg," she said one afternoon when I walked into her room on the seventh floor to find her shades drawn, the room dark and gloomy. "I don't deserve this."

"I know," I said. I took her hand and I held it, but there wasn't much else to say; often, God does not feel faithful when you are in the midst of despair, and, as William Munny (Clint Eastwood) tells a man about to die in *Unforgiven*, "Deserves got nothing to do with it." Many times there is not a correlation between what we do and what happens to us, even though many of our sacred and secular narratives insist there is.

It just doesn't make sense. And that's one of the things that may have prompted Marvella's feelings of despair; as McIntyre notes, the sense that "an intelligible narrative in which one was playing a part" has turned into "a story of unintelligible episodes" almost always leads to our experiencing despair and pain.[8]

Marvella's despair was not just a loss of faith in God, although for a while she had her doubts there, and she certainly was having a hard time making sense of the story of God she'd carried around until then. But it was also a loss of faith in the larger contract she thought she had with existence, in the stories she had thought she occupied. She had listened to her doctors. She was a good person. She deserved to be well and happy. Why wasn't she?

These stories of progress are insidious, because they are reinforced by everything from American popular culture (Be thin and happy!) to popular religion (God *wants* you to be thin and happy!). Barbara Brown Taylor has preached that Americans do not know how to suffer—we know how to relieve, it, how to evade it, but not how to confront it (and certainly not how to accept it).[9] When you accept as your due that you are supposed to be happy, then unhappiness makes—literally—no sense. And as I keep repeating, the primary practical function of stories is to help us make sense of our lives.

So here's the problem: all of these secular stories tend to crack open at unhappiness.

And grief and suffering can simply smash them to pieces.

Take, for example, the story of Mark, the Texas state trooper who showed up badly hurt in the ER one morning after an accident on a rural road in the Hill Country. The representative of a just society, a beloved father and husband, he deserved happiness if anyone deserves happiness. And yet, there he was in one of the crash bays, unconscious, bleeding, and the focus of attention of both his care team and a body of worried state troopers in the waiting room that grew so large during the day that by the time Mark was officially admitted and moved up to intensive care, the MICU charge nurse asked me to go out and make sure they knew that they had to stay in the lobby.

Mark was our star patient that morning, and not only because of the troopers in the waiting room. He was our representative of a life lived right, a life worth saving, and although I never saw a patient the staff and doctors didn't try to help, Mark drew our finest care and our most careful attention.

Mark survived his injuries, and I had the joy of bringing his worried wife back to greet him after he woke up from his surgery—and of announcing to more state troopers than I had seen before or ever want to see again that their friend was going to live. But lots of others—even those who might have deserved good fortune—were not so fortunate that summer. And what was I to say to them and those who loved them?

Faith in Science and Medicine

The narrator of P. D. James's novel *The Children of Men* is a pretty sharp character who looks around at the future world humans have created, a world very much like ours, and observes, "Western science has been our god. . . . It has preserved, comforted, healed, warmed, fed, and entertained us."[10] Like us, the people in his world hope against hope that science will solve every problem, cure every ill. And for those who are suffering with ailments or conditions, that faith in science can be startlingly real.

Pamela, the woman I told you about with terminal brain cancer, really wanted to do God's will, whatever that might be—to live, to die, to be faithful to a miraculous hope. I could see that in the passion of her prayer, and in her calmer moments, in her eyes. But at the same time, the picture that emerged from her charts, her doctors and nurses, and her conversations with me revealed to me that while she might love and revere God, her primary faith was in modern medicine. My notes on her case, which I shared verbatim with my colleagues, went like this:

> I've been working with a patient who is devoutly Christian, and full of Jesus talk, but who has become so scared of leaving the hospital that she has put off her release for five days

now. What this is making me think of is that while we may have a powerful faith in God, our society has also encouraged us to have a powerful faith in medicine—and the two of them may clash, as they seem to be doing here. In each of our times together she has told me that she wants to trust in God and she wants to release control, but checking the nurses' notes she seems to be very very involved in demanding certain drugs, and in demanding that the doctors be called in the middle of the night—which was when I first saw her, since she had demanded that the on-call chaplain come to Brack immediately.

So, very high intensity patient, the nurses just want her to go home—and she won't. The charge nurse says she's terminal, and the doctors have been upfront about her possibilities. I just think she feels safer in the hospital, more in control, somehow.

I was present one afternoon a few days later when her doctors came huddled in a group to talk to Pamela. You might imagine that strictly from humanitarian concerns it would be appropriate to let a patient stay on after her or his medical needs are taken care of, but hospitals don't actually work this way. Even if you put economic concerns aside, the press of available beds was a daily problem at Brackenridge, where there were always sicker patients in ER waiting for a bed in ICU, and ICU patients needing to be moved to regular beds. Hospitals are not hotels with medical staff attached—they are intended to be used by the sickest people, the ones who will most benefit from being there.

And Pamela not only wasn't benefiting from being there, she was keeping someone else from benefiting as well.

So Pamela's doctors spoke with her softly and slowly, as you might speak to a young child. Her lead doctor, who was from Pakistan or India, told her, "We have arranged for you to receive at home the medical care you have been receiving here. There is no longer a reason for you to be here. I am signing your discharge."

He did, with a flourish like an exclamation point.

And you would have thought from the expression of panic on her face that he was signing her death notice.

After they left, I tried to console her, to bring her back to the idea of faith she had expressed to me on a number of occasions. At that moment, she wasn't having any of it.

"I thought they would understand," she said, shaking her head, and not looking up at me. "I thought they would understand."

What did she want them to understand? Well, what she was expressing, whether she realized it or not, was her underlying belief: "If I leave the hospital, I will die."

God's will, whatever it might be, had fallen by the wayside. Now there was nothing but her faith in the hospital and its staff to administer a healing miracle that might keep her going for another day, month, year.

I found this unthinking but absolute faith in medicine in many of the people I encountered that summer. For better or worse, they believed that if only the doctors would isolate a correct diagnosis and prescribe a regimen of treatment, a person— they, their loved one—could be healed. A person could even be snatched back from the jaws of death, if only the system would go to work.

I talked to Andy's mom, Deb, in the waiting room outside the Brackenridge MICU, where she was waiting with Andy's girlfriend Carlene for visiting hours to begin, and although she was happy for me to pray with them, she was angry with Brackenridge.

It turned out that Andy (like many Brack patients) didn't have medical insurance, and Deb was convinced that the staff hadn't bothered to stop his intestinal bleeding because he couldn't pay for his care.

"It just burns me up," Deb said, her face flushing. "I know they can figure out what's wrong with him and fix him up. I just know it, Father. [This was a frequent misidentification; by this time, I had stopped trying to correct it.] And they won't because we can't pay 'em. It's prejudice, pure and simple."

I let it sit for a second, acknowledged what she had said, then gently tried to prompt her in another direction.

"Deb," I told her, "Look around this room. Hardly anyone in here has insurance. The doctors are doing the best they can for everyone. If someone in my family was sick, this is where I would bring them." All of which was true enough. But none of my assurances that his doctors were doing their very best—or about all the other patients who didn't have health insurance—made any difference to her. It was an item of faith: modern medicine could fix Andy, if it chose to.

It just didn't choose to.

This absolute faith in technology to save us and medicine to heal us is part of a worldview that Stanley Hauerwas connects to this larger myth of progress: We adopt this medical narrative of meaning because we live in a world "that promises to 'solve' suffering by eliminating its causes."[11] This "medicalization" of our stories limits our abilities to develop coherent explanatory narratives outside of the medical narrative because it treats human beings as patients with problems to be solved and expresses a belief that sickness and death are always inadequate endings to their narratives.

Medicalization does not make allowances for the larger life stories in which sickness and suffering might become not only understandable but the keys to new self-knowledge or knowledge of God. "What bothers us about illness," Hauerwas notes, "is not simply the pain and suffering that it occasions, but the absurdity of it."[12] The patient is not, in other words, just seeking relief from an ailment or injury; she or he is seeking meaning, understanding, wholeness, a story that makes sense. Perhaps the illness is even a part of that meaning, that movement toward wholeness. Pastoral counselor and seminary professor Dan Bagby observes how "each personal journey is a sacred story that needs telling. So part of a counselor's contribution is 'witnessing to the telling' of someone's story, and often acknowledging—validating—that person's life, along with the injustices, sufferings, betrayals, and hopes connected to that life."[13]

Ideally, that is what should happen to help patients and grieving onlookers make some sense of things. But Hauerwas notes that our doctors and medical workers have been trained to delay the end of life, not to help patients understand how their illnesses and deaths might be an essential part of those lives.[14] And, John Polkinghorne says, the problem gets even more extreme: our belief in medical and scientific solutions has become for some a sort of "medical eschatology," a hope-myth that suggests that death may someday (at least, for those who can afford it) become optional.[15] Why bother trying to understand your death or illness if you can simply put it off indefinitely?

But the scientific/medical narrative falls to pieces because it cannot embrace an idea of wholeness that might come through illness or injury; neither can it accept the inevitability of death. In a medical narrative, when doctors can't solve a problem, arrest a disease, or stop a person from dying, then absurdity is the only possible result; there is no way to create a whole and coherent story from medical failure when length and continuance of life are absolute values.

Nor can the medical narrative deal well with the idea that life should not necessarily be continued in all cases. Hauerwas calls this secular belief that life can (and should) be prolonged to the limits of medical science "chronicity."[16] Everyone is supposed to live, if not forever, then for a long, long time.

While we Americans heartily seek health and wholeness through medicine and technology and may even faithfully believe in its ability to extend our lives indefinitely, sometimes, despite the best efforts of medical personnel, people still die; cancer will spread; hearts will stop. Tragedy does not skip Americans just because they have an intense belief in happiness and Marcus Welby, MD.

Nor does grief pass like the avenging spirit of the Lord over those who consciously or unconsciously believe that money *can* buy happiness. Andy's story—or, perhaps, Andy's mom's story—also suggests an American corollary, that we live our lives in the shapes of American stories of capitalism and transaction.

Simply put, we live in a society where we are encouraged to believe that we can buy our way to happiness and purchase happy endings.

The Myth of Consumerism

Thomas Merton once wrote that he happily left society for the monastery because he could not accept the stories it tried to foist upon him—what he called "servitudes to certain standards of value that to me were idiotic and repugnant . . . a society that is happy because it drinks Coca-Cola or Seagrams or both."[17] Update Merton's examples to include Hummers and McMansions, iPods and satellite radio, and you can see that we remain in a society in which happiness is—purportedly—measured by our ability to consume.[18] So, perhaps, is meaning. A 2007 story in the *Economist* makes the far-too-apposite suggestion that shopping has replaced faith in God in many places in the Western world, that people are meeting their spiritual needs—or seeking to—through shopping.[19] Certainly more Westerners today worship regularly in the narthex of shopping malls than in their local churches, and the American punk/pop band Green Day sang with far too much prescience about "the holy scriptures of a shopping mall" in their song "Jesus of Suburbia."

Simply put, our ability to buy what we want to think we need has become a simple item of faith for us, but the problem comes because, as Jesus said, "Where your treasure is, there your heart will be also" (Luke 12:34).

Each product we buy is packaged to appeal to the myth that buying it will make us happy: buy this car, that perfume, this house in that neighborhood. Still, it doesn't take much human understanding to realize that this narrative is built on a platform of human greed on both sides of the equation, and rare indeed are those who have succeeded in buying happiness.[20] Merton made use of the Greek myth of Tantalus (who resides in hell, where the fruit above him and the water below him always recede beyond his hand when he reaches out for them—hence our word "tantalizing") to explain how the American story of consumerism actually functions:

> If we are fools enough to remain at the mercy of the people who want to sell us happiness, it will be impossible for us ever

to be content with anything. How would they profit if we became content? . . . The last thing the salesman wants is for the buyer to become content. You are of no use in our affluent society unless you are always just about to grasp what you never have.

The Greeks were not as smart as we are. In their primitive way they put Tantalus in hell. Madison Avenue, on the contrary, would convince us that Tantalus is in heaven.[21]

And yet for all our recognitions of what money cannot buy, we seem to have a genuine attachment to the idea that there are some things it assuredly can buy. This was Deb's mistake when she bemoaned her son Andy's illness; underlying her words was this unspoken assumption: "We are poor," she was telling me. "If we could afford good medical coverage, my son would be well by now. Andy is getting worse only because we can't buy his good health."

This combination of faith in medical science—and in the almighty dollar—is one of the most lethal combinations in American life. It is one of the factors that has led to the skyrocketing cost of American health care relative to that of other industrialized nations, and to a massive preponderance of care at the end of life, where we struggle medically to stave off death, since it is an inappropriate ending for the American story—and because we can afford it.

Or can we? Julie Appleby reported in *USA Today* that more than a fourth of all Medicare spending—that is, more than a quarter of Medicare's $327 billion budget—is spent on treatment for patients in the last year of their lives. Sometimes this care is appropriate, and sometimes it's wasteful. She notes that

Across the nation, some patients spend much of their final weeks seeing specialists, having tests, trying new drugs. Many die attached to machines, such as ventilators, in hospitals.

For some patients, that's exactly the right care. Doing everything that can be done to save an 18-year-old motorcycle-crash victim makes sense. But what about an 85-year-old with

heart failure, diabetes and cancer? Do you continue aggres-
sive chemotherapy?[22]

Well, we often do, because our faith in medicine and in spending allows no alternative. But there is an alternative. I think often
about Verne, a gay street person ravaged with AIDS, who asked
me to come up to his room in Brackenridge to talk with him about
advanced directives, the instructions patients are allowed to give
the hospital about their end-of-life preferences. After I read him
the alternatives about emergency treatment and talked about
them with him, Verne asked to sign a "Do not resuscitate" (DNR)
order; in the absence of such an order, the doctors and nurses will
always attempt to resuscitate a patient who has coded, using whatever tools and techniques they have at hand.

People cannot be permitted simply to *die*.[23]

But simply dying was exactly what Verne wanted, and he told
me so. "I just want to die with a little dignity," he said quietly. "My
life has been hard enough. I don't want a three-ring circus at the
end of it."

To be sure, time and time again I saw heroic efforts being made
on behalf of someone whose life could not be saved, only prolonged, and often without much quality of life. It is, as we will discover later, indeed different to talk about resuscitating an
eighteen-year-old accident victim as opposed to an eighty-year-
old suffering from end-of-life conditions, but our belief in the
medical and consumer stories often doesn't make this differentia-
tion: every life must be saved—again and again, if possible. I was
called to the sides of several patients who had coded, and coded
again, resuscitated for a bit even though there was little or no
prospect for their recovery.

What is a respectful stopping point, a place where we might say
that death is a natural process and it's OK to permit it?

We'll consider some of our stories about death in chapter 4, but
we can say here that as long as our story looks at death as failure
that can and should be staved off by medical intervention, as long
as we think throwing money at a problem will solve it, then we
will continue to view death as defeat.

And, for Americans, defeat is something we simply cannot make room for in our stories.

The Myth of Power

I had seen the Colonel on the MICU ward for several days before he coded. Although I never saw him conscious, I knew from his charts, my meetings with his nurses, and my observation that he was a retired Air Force officer in his eighties, a big man with a barrel chest that had sagged closer to his midsection as the years passed. He was still an imposing figure, even recumbent, and I could imagine him as the war hero his family told me about who had flown in World War II, Korea, and Vietnam.

I was on call the night he coded in MICU, and I met with his most recent wife. She was at least thirty years his junior, about the age of his oldest son, with whom she stood waiting in the sixth-floor visitors' area. They both seemed to regard the fact that the Colonel's heart had stopped as impossible, an anomaly; he had never given up before, and he certainly wasn't going to do so now.

Failure was simply not an option where the Colonel was concerned.

I traveled back and forth between the ICU and the family, and as the medical team continued to work on the Colonel, I wanted to prepare his wife and son, because it didn't look good. A trick my friends Hunt and Roger had taught me from their chaplaincy days was to use the phrase "the sickest person in this hospital." To tell someone, "Right now, your husband is the sickest person in this hospital," usually helps to prepare people if things continue to get worse.

So that night, I told the Colonel's wife and son, "Right now, he's the sickest person in Brackenridge."

And they didn't even blink. The smile didn't leave his wife's face. Because he was the Colonel. He was tough, he was strong, and he could defeat anything. He always had. And I think at least part of them believed he always would.

So when he died in the ICU after coding a second time (and I have to say, when the Colonel did something, he really did go all out; I have never seen a person who looked as dead as that man when he was all done), their faith in a story of power collapsed, and they were left with nothing. When I looked into their eyes, I could see that they were lost. They were not people of faith—or what they had had faith in was the Colonel always being there. And now, they didn't know what to believe.

When I told my sister-in-law Marcy, who is an ICU nurse, about this case, she nodded knowingly. "It's like whatever they were standing on got pulled out from under them," she said. She had seen it many times herself. "And now they're just free-falling."

A belief in power is compelling, and seductive, for Americans hold power that no other people in the history of the world have known: the ability to consume a lion's share of the world's resources, the largest outlay on defense of any nation, such prolific economic resources that even members of the American middle class are fabulously wealthy by the standards of much of the rest of the world.

A theology of weakness—what some theologians have called a "theology of the cross"—advocates that, like Jesus (or like God, in the person of Jesus), we give ourselves up to the events of this life, not seeking to avoid pain, but opening ourselves to the belief that God can transform the events of our lives—even the painful ones—into something sacred.

Karl Rahner and Herbert Vorgrimler end their theological definition of power by saying that not only is God's power directly in opposition to the drive of individuals or institutions toward taking and holding power, but that "the final consequence of Jesus' message of the reconciliatory rule or kingdom of God was his acceptance of death on the cross."[24] Henri Nouwen goes a step further. He argues that not only did God choose powerlessness as the vehicle for our redemption, but that God weeps to see us grasp at power, because this desire separates us from God and each other, and that when we seek power, "our lives become *diabolic*, in the literal meaning of the word: *divisive*."[25]

As we will see in more detail later, the Gospel of John, which presents a version of Christ who is already God when he goes up on the cross, tells us that God does actually choose to be sacrificed, even though he could control events, even though he could alter history. As Jack Miles describes it, in this choice, God is electing to renounce a long-standing status as a warrior on the physical plane (the God of Battles who has fought for political and historical victory) and has decided instead to become a spiritual savior. Thus, all of sacred history has led to this moment of weakness and suffering that will be transformed, paradoxically, into cosmic victory, for God, and for us.[26]

Notice that a theology of weakness is not the same as *being* weak; far from it. But a theology of sacred weakness is totally at odds with many of the things we seem to believe, judging by our actions.

Many of us adhere to a theology of power—something like what Martin Luther used to call a "Theology of Empire"—that expects God to uphold us in all we do, that enshrines our choices and desires as holy writ. In Jim Wallis's words, this sort of theology "invokes God's blessing on our activities, agendas, and purposes."[27] (In other words, "God, get on board with what I want, because I know best.")

That is dangerous when we do it as a nation, and it is also dangerous when we do it as individuals. True faith requires opening ourselves to the possibility that our plans for our lives do not necessarily represent God's plans for us, however inconvenient or painful that recognition might be. It requires trusting that, whatever our stories about God, our creator loves and cares for us. And when we do this, as Nouwen noted of himself, "something beyond my expectations begins to happen for me."[28]

Something beyond, and in the plan of God, something even better.

To be a Christian is to stand against the cultural stories of power, affluence, and visibility; it is, as Nouwen argues, to choose "downward mobility" as the true path of Christ, since power, success, fame, money, and all the other pursuits that seem so important for us now cannot satisfy us or bring peace. Only when we renounce these false stories, these false ambitions, can we know fulfillment.[29]

Still, I know it's difficult to renounce power, particularly for a people like ourselves who have so many resources and are so used to power. I couldn't tell you, for instance, where the Colonel's widow and son wound up spiritually; our primary discussion after the Colonel's death centered not on their grief and loss, but on a much more practical matter, deciding what funeral home they should contact. They looked over the list together, they discussed pros and cons.

They made the call.

Their eyes were still vacant when they disappeared into the elevators, but they did seem a little more at ease once they'd made arrangements for the Colonel's body to be picked up.

It was, at least, something that they could pay for, an element of this tragedy they could control.

And that was the story they had been living in all along.

The Comfort of Nothingness

This is not where I hoped we would end up, and it is certainly not where hope leads us. But it seems clear that if Robin Griffith-Jones was right about the responses of Mary and Martha to their brother's death—that both hope and despair are possibilities—we must acknowledge, then, the belief in a story where life is essentially formless and meaningless as a final secular narrative that people employ to create meaning.

Charlie was one of the homeless patients I met when I was doing rounds on the eighth-floor chronic care ward. The nurses had called me to see him several times because he was a troublemaker. He wouldn't stay in his room. He liked to wander the hallways. He argued with the staff about his care, about the doses, about the diagnoses.

I saw Charlie on several occasions in the hospital that summer, but on this one, he was in with a broken leg. Two nights ago, he had stepped or fallen in front of a moving car, which had hit him and shattered his leg. He was in a cast up past his hip, and even the pain medication couldn't make him feel very good about life, although since he was an alcoholic, the hospital was giving him Miller beer to keep him from going through withdrawal.

I tried to follow my usual routine when I met Charlie, who was sitting irritably in his chair after his nurse had told him that if he left his room again, she'd have him thrown out of the hospital. So he was in a bad mood when I got there. But I don't think it did much more than flavor his delivery. I sensed that he would have had the same things to say to me even on a better day.

"How'm I feeling?" he asked in response to my question. "It's over, man. Just what you'd expect."

The eighth-floor social worker was trying to track down his Social Security check, but he didn't have much hope that it would happen. "I'll be dead by then," he said, taking a sip of his beer, then grimacing at the taste. "Not that it matters."

He held the can for a moment, looked at it reflectively, held it this way and that so the fluorescent light glinted off of it.

"Not that anything matters," he said, and took another drink.

Sometimes, particularly in a life that has been painted in broad strokes of heartbreak, people come to believe that the meaning of their lives can best be explained by a story that life is meaningless. For people who dwell in this land where nothing matters, nothing creates, nothing upholds, the words of one of Ernest Hemingway's narrators resonate powerfully:

> What did he fear? It was not fear or dread. It was a nothing that he knew too well. It was all a nothing and a man was nothing too. . . . Hail nothing full of nothing, nothing is with thee.[30]

If some supreme being is not going to intervene on behalf of the good and punish the evil, if one's actions don't seem to have an immediate or even eventual effect on one's fate, if there isn't some readily discerned ultimate meaning, then it's easy to believe that we live in an indifferent universe where we are all alone to make up our own meaning as best we can. It's easy to simply give up and refuse to attach a larger meaning to why some people live and others die, to why there is pain and suffering. There just is, because that is all there is.

The American writer Stephen Crane wrote a poem about the relationship between human beings and the cosmos that has been in my head since I first heard it as an undergraduate:

> A man said to the universe:
> 'Sir, I exist.'
> 'However,' replied the universe,
> 'The fact has not created in me
> A sense of obligation.'[31]

American literary naturalism, the literary school to which Crane belonged, flourished at the end of the nineteenth and turn of the twentieth centuries, but the feelings of emptiness and hopelessness that sometimes infuse these stories, poems, and novels is still alive and well. In the work of Crane, Theodore Dreiser, Jack London, and Edith Wharton, we find stories in which people live out their lives in clear knowledge that their choices are not part of a larger meaning, that they live or die purely by whim in a universe depopulated of meaning, that, to quote the title of a long-ago album by John Mellencamp, "Nothin' Matters and What If It Did."

The narrator of Crane's short story "The Open Boat" says, in a moment of great trauma,

> When it occurs to a man that nature does not regard him as important, and that she feels she would not maim the universe by disposing of him, he at first wishes to throw bricks at the temple, and he hates deeply the fact that there are no bricks and no temples.[32]

What he describes in this passage is a haunting and empty world, but it's a world that many people who have given up believing would recognize. There seems little proof of the temple, let alone of something worth offering praise and sacrifice to within its nonexistent walls. In too many of our lives, our needs and desires have seemed to go so unnoticed that it is simply easier to believe in nothing, to stop hoping for meaning.

To stop hoping, period.

I recently got a disturbing e-mail from Trent, an old friend of mine from New Orleans I had been out of contact with during my years of holding down a full-time teaching job while doing full-time seminary studies. We had been out of touch, in fact, since before Katrina. He was on my heart, so I had asked how he was doing, how things had been since the hurricane and floods. His reply chilled me.

Katrina and its bungled aftermath had been horrible, he said, the chaos, the fear, four feet of water standing in his home, four months before they could move back in, and then they did so without water or electricity. But what happened after was even worse—the collapse of his beloved city, the collapse of his business. He had been forced to lay off almost a hundred employees, including many who had been promised job security, and I knew that all of these events had been immensely painful to him because I knew and loved the person he is.

Trent used to proudly define himself as an intellectual and artistic person of faith, a subgroup that often seems so small that we grasp for as many coconspirators as we can find. But after summarizing the travails of the past few years, he wrote, "I have a lot of anger and a crushing feeling of the aimlessness of all things."

In this statement, Trent expresses a point of view that I myself harbored at times over the years when my best attempts to make sense of life failed, when my best stories had been overturned. In the days of my worst depression and the failure of my relationships, I felt I was waving hard at the universe (since I didn't have a brick to throw), yelling, "Hey, I'm alive over here."

And the universe was saying, in return, "So what? Who cares? Have a mouthful of dirt."

Nobody likes it when the universe doesn't respond to our needs. There's a standing joke in my family about the fact that my father used to say "God hates me" in response to disasters large and small.

If his car didn't start, "God hates me."

If we were sailing out in the middle of the lake and the wind died down, "God hates me."

It might be a little bit intoxicating to imagine that the ruler of the universe is actively involved in your life, even if that involvement is primarily negative. But what we are talking about in the sort of nihilistic story that Charlie and Trent are telling for us is the belief that there is no higher power actively involved in your life, that nothing in this life matters beyond the moment, and it's better to accept that now because it'll be easier, at least, than living in false hope.

It is a conscious decision to live in a story of despair because despair is the only story that seems to make sense in a world filled with unsolved pain and suffering, and sometimes living without hope seems, paradoxically, like the best we can hope for.

But, thank God, our faith traditions suggest that there are other answers to pain, other stories about suffering that might open new understandings for us, and it is to those stories that we will turn our attention now.

Chapter Three

"I Love the Psalms"

Stories of Grief from the Hebrew Bible

Before the mountains were brought forth, or ever you had formed the earth and the world, from everlasting to everlasting you are God.

Ps. 90:2

Marvella was both a theological treasure trove and important to me personally during my summer in the hospital; we had a long-running relationship—rare in itself in a hospital where typically people vanished quickly and new patients with new complaints replaced them—and her illness took so many twists and turns that she grappled with a number of issues—and forced me to wrestle with them alongside her. Early on, I got a clear sense of where Marvella's comfort came from. During that first visit, when I came to bring her a Bible, she asked if I would read something to her, and her choice, as you'll remember, was Psalm 121:

> I lift up my eyes to the hills—
>   from where will my help come?
> My help comes from the LORD,
>   who made heaven and earth.
>   (vv. 1–2)

She listened with satisfaction (as who would not), sighing a "Yes, Lord" here and there, and when I was done reading, she lay contentedly for a moment. It's not that I was such a great reader; it's that these verses were a real source of comfort to her, her affirmation that everything was going to be well.

"I love the Psalms," she said, at last, almost purring in the midst of her pain and discomfort, and I could understand what she meant. When you hear psalms like that one, spoken out of what we assume to be a situation of distress and moving into a story of sure healing and wholeness, it's clear why we are so often drawn to them in times of trial. I myself have felt the healing touch of certain psalms.

But ultimately, as we will discover, the psalms—and the Hebrew Scriptures at large—tell a more complicated and also richer story of suffering than the simple expectation that God is going to fix everything to our satisfaction.[1] We will look at this compelling story. But we'll also see that the Hebrew Scriptures teach us that the entire scope of human understanding—including loss, grief, and anger—are under God.

But let's begin with the psalms of comfort, since they fit so well into the stories we have been telling—the stories in which things will be all right because we are Christian, or American, or have resources, or have done everything we think we are supposed to have done—and so on. These psalms, even when they acknowledge life's difficulty and sadness, typically pick us up and place us back on our feet again, and certainly that's what we would prefer.

For Marvella, Psalm 121 was a marvelous promise in the midst of her pain. Marvella thought that she knew what was best for her—that she quickly get out of the hospital and back to her work for the Lord, and I think she felt that God knew that too. When she heard the psalmist say that God would watch over her and be her help, she had a definite idea what that meant: God was coming to intervene in her illness, to heal her, and to return her to the life she had lived—which was the best life she could imagine.

And so it is with many of the psalms. As Bernhard W. Anderson and Steven Bishop point out in the book *Out of the Depths: The Psalms Speak for Us Today*, both the psalms of praise and the psalms of lament are centered on the idea that God either has intervened or can intervene in human difficulty.[2] Unlike some of the Christian stories of healing we will look at later, the psalms fit into a very definite pattern of formal lament found in the Hebrew Bible. As Anderson and Bishop note, "the laments found in Jeremiah's confessions, the book of Job, and Lamentations have the same general form as the laments found in the Psalter."[3]

Their promise—or hope—of intervention is totally this-worldly. The psalmists—and the other writers of Hebrew lament—believe God is acting in what Erich Zenger calls God's part in the temporal "back-and-forth between chaos and cosmos," what Anderson and Bishop define as God's relationship with human beings in this life, expressed entirely in the context of our life here and now.[4] So in many ways, this "Old Testament" understanding of God and God's intervening hand fits well with some of the secular narratives believed by American Christians. The psalms of praise and hopeful lament make a place for suffering—it is real, and it is a part of life—but they simultaneously suggest that God will intervene in a timely fashion *in this life* to repair the damage that the world, the powers, or even God may have done to us.[5] Although we will discuss the body of the book of Job in more detail, it is this impulse—making things right in a temporal fashion—that helps explain the seemingly tacked-on ending of Job, where God intervenes to give that sufferer a new family, new farms, and a new life, although it seems to contradict the ultimate spiritual understanding of the book:

> And the LORD restored the fortunes of Job when he had prayed for his friends; and the LORD gave Job twice as much as he had before. . . . The LORD blessed the latter days of Job more than his beginning; and he had fourteen thousand sheep, six thousand camels, a thousand yoke of oxen, and a thousand donkeys. (Job 42:10, 12)

As the ending of Job and certain of the psalms suggest, these Hebrew writers held a view of justice and faithfulness very similar to the one many of us still hold today: If God does not move to make things right in this life, it is as though God does not move at all.

So the psalms of lament (and other Hebrew laments) and the psalms of praise suggest to us that God can and does actively intervene in the life of the world to make things right again. They also suggest that there are definitely things that need to be made right, that suffering and adversity are a part of this existence. But faith in God will ultimately carry us into a life that will be blessed by God—a blessed life in this world, witnessed by others. And it will be, we often presume, a life very similar to what we imagine our best life now might be.

The best known of the psalms, of course, beloved by Jews and Christians alike, is Psalm 23, a psalm of David. During my summer as a chaplain, I often recited it myself on the way to a Code Blue, as I drove to an on-call, or as I rode up in the elevator in the hospital to begin doing rounds. I am a shy person under the best of circumstances, and the idea of walking into a setting full of strangers in the midst of great trauma almost always carried some trepidation with it. So the familiar verses were like a comforting mantra, reminding me that I was not going anywhere that God did not walk with me:

> The LORD is my shepherd, I shall not want.
>   He makes me lie down in green pastures;
> he leads me beside still waters;
>   he restores my soul.
> He leads me in right paths
>   for his name's sake.
>
> Even though I walk through the darkest valley,
>   I fear no evil;
> for you are with me;
>   your rod and your staff—
>   they comfort me.
>
> You prepare a table before me
>   in the presence of my enemies;
> you anoint my head with oil;
>   my cup overflows.

Surely goodness and mercy shall follow me
   all the days of my life,
and I shall dwell in the house of the LORD
   my whole life long.

         (Ps. 23:1–6)

Before I exited the elevator and put on my chaplain's face, I would cross myself, repeat to myself silently, "I will fear no evil, for you are with me," and off I would go. I also remembered how—as with Marvella and her psalm—the Twenty-Third Psalm had been a balm during the dark times when I myself had been a sojourner in the darkest valley, the valley of the shadow of death.

I've written elsewhere that hope is a necessary quality for life, and during the times my depression dragged me farthest down, I had no hope that anything worthwhile could ever change my life for the better. I had exhausted almost every avenue of hope; I was certainly incapable of it, and while my family and friends loved me, they couldn't hope for me. At last, as I came to a faith that was strong, vital, and the only thing keeping me on the planet, I called out to God for help—even though most days I couldn't see any difference in the way I felt, loved, or lived. But that point is a significant one: No matter how bad things got, even when I saw no immediate result, I called out to God—I lifted my eyes to the hills.

And I hoped beyond hope that my help would come.

These prayers—at first feeble, then fervent—were expressions of my faith in a loving God; as Anderson and Bishop note of the psalms, they were "expressions of praise offered in a minor key in the confidence that Yahweh is faithful."[6] I couldn't know for certain that God would rescue me from the morass (from out of the depths, as in the great Psalm 130, associated by Chrysostom and other early Christians with despair), but I knew that my only hope was that God would do so.

It is here—in the psalms' acknowledgment that perhaps God isn't simply like a light switch we flick, a gumball machine we put a quarter in—that they do us perhaps their greatest service. Some of the psalms, after all, not only start in a bad place, but remain there. They don't take us to a land of milk and honey—or show

us goodness and mercy following all the days of our lives. Sometimes they simply cry out—a voice calling for help, feeble, and
maybe even futile—in the direction of God. As Dietrich Bonhoeffer wrote in his tiny book about praying the psalms, in many of
them there is no "quick and easy" acceptance of suffering, but
rather, "always struggle, anxiety, doubt." Yet even in the most
hopeless situations, "God alone remains the one addressed."[7]

The psalms—the difficult as well as the comforting—provide a
powerful corrective for a typical American Christianity, what
Walter Brueggemann calls (and we should now recognize as) a
Christian faith that is romantic in its belief that everything in this
life will work out for the best.[8] The "Psalms of Disorientation" (as
Brueggemann calls them) remind us that even when we don't see
the hand of God reaching down to pull us to safety, who else is
there to cry to?

When David's son became sick (in 2 Samuel, this illness is
described as God's judgment against David's sins, although I hope
this is a story we're learning to question), this writer of psalms
throws himself on the ground, fasts, and for seven days, prays to
God for the life of his son.

And at the end of that time his son dies, all the same.

What is there to do? God's hand was not stayed; light did not
break into the darkness.

But who else is there to cry to? So David rises up from the news
of his son's death, cleans and dresses himself, and goes into the
house of the Eternal God to worship.

The Psalms of Disorientation also remind us that life doesn't
always make sense in a way that we can apprehend rationally.
Brueggemann's influential division of the book of Psalms into
three groups helps us here: Psalms of Orientation (everything is
all right); Psalms of Disorientation (everything is all wrong); and
Psalms of New Orientation (everything is all wrong, but it will be
all right).[9] When we are in the midst of suffering, we are most
grateful for the first and last, for these are the hopeful psalms. But
we should also be grateful for those that are most disruptive to our
understanding of God—the Psalms of Disorientation that suggest
that sometimes there are no easy answers, that sometimes God

does not swoop down like Superman and save the day—at least, in this life. Suffering, as we have said, disorients us until we can find a story in which it makes sense, but these difficult Psalms of Disorientation help us to understand that there are stories in which suffering persists—but so does faith.

Although I often read the psalms to people during that summer, there was one other occasion in which they played a major—and unexpected—part in my exchanges with a patient. On one of my visits with Pamela, the devout woman with the inoperable brain tumor, she asked me to read to her. On that occasion, I felt strongly led (perhaps because of the opening line "Lord, you have been our dwelling place") to read her Psalm 90, a psalm that Brueggemann names as one of the Psalms of Disorientation. You may remember that Pamela had struggled with the seriousness of her illness, with her fears, with her desire to remain in the hospital, and with her desire to do God's will, whatever that might be. As I read further, we discovered together that many of these things were addressed by the psalm:

> Lord, you have been our dwelling place
> in all generations.
> Before the mountains were brought forth,
> or ever you had formed the earth and the world,
> from everlasting to everlasting you are God.
>
> You turn us back to dust,
> and say, "Turn back, you mortals."
> For a thousand years in your sight
> are like yesterday when it is past,
> or like a watch in the night.
>
> You sweep them away; they are like a dream,
> like grass that is renewed in the morning;
> in the morning it flourishes and is renewed;
> in the evening it fades and withers.
>
> For we are consumed by your anger;
> by your wrath we are overwhelmed.

You have set our iniquities before you,
    our secret sins in the light of your countenance.

For all our days pass away under your wrath;
    our years come to an end like a sigh.
The days of our life are seventy years,
    or perhaps eighty, if we are strong;
even then their span is only toil and trouble;
    they are soon gone, and we fly away.

                          (Ps. 90:1–10)

Only by a stretch of the interpretive imagination can we suggest that anything like affirmation and healing come in these verses, yet as I read, and after, Pamela closed her eyes, nodded her head, and wept. To hear these words—that God is God and that we are only human, that our days are limited, and that perhaps the most we can hope for is wisdom to know that—in some unaccountable way, these terrifically challenging lines soothed her.

When we talked about this psalm, she said that it gave her courage to let go, if letting go was required, and to struggle hard, if that was what she needed to do. The final lines of the psalm (v. 17: "Let the favor of the Lord our God be upon us, and prosper for us the work of our hands—O prosper the work of our hands!") about the work we are capable of doing spoke to her about continuing to do her part for as long as she was able. These are words about our faithful relationship to a faithful God, and our faithfulness to the tasks we have been given to do. Everything else is out of our control. As Brueggemann writes, "we would not have expected the psalm to end with this [the works of our hands]. Indeed, the psalm would seem to be a dismissal of such concerns" in favor of the cosmic works of God's hands.[10] But as Brueggemann notices, this psalm ends with hope—the hope that God will value what we do even in our human weakness, that God will still be "our God." Even if healing isn't found, that relationship between us continues.

Elie Wiesel tells of how, when he was fifteen, he was among religious Jews in Auschwitz who had cried out for help and yet found no relief from their suffering.[11] At last, three rabbis put God on trial for neglect, for failing to live up to the covenant with the Jews. Speakers on both sides presented their cases, God was excoriated and defended, and at last, by vote of the assembly, God was found guilty.

And then they all, prosecutors and defenders, like David praying after the death of his child, went off to observe Shabbat.

God had not answered their prayers, they all remained in deadly danger, and most of them would die in that horrible place, yet they continued to pray. How many of us would demonstrate that sort of faithfulness?

It reminds me of a story about a patient in the MICU at Brackenridge, of the only time that summer when I actually felt fear. Teresa, the charge nurse, a no-nonsense woman who really knew her stuff, had asked me to visit her isolation patient Shoshannna, a forty-five-year-old African American woman who was suffering from just about every communicable disease and physical disorder I could imagine: she had hepatitis C, cirrhosis, and hypertension; she was HIV-positive. Judging by her long list of conditions, she was or had been an IV-drug user and possibly a prostitute; some religious folks might have suggested that she was suffering the wages of sin and figured she could suffer them just fine without their help. Now I never felt any such thing—I've committed some pretty spectacular sins in my time—but there was still a long moment when I hesitated outside the door after I was gloved, masked, and gowned, not because I looked down on Shoshanna in any way, but because her condition was so serious, her diseases so ominous.

Although we wore masks and gowns when we worked with people who were highly contagious, I had worked with comparatively few patients during the summer who were so critically ill; since Brack was a trauma hospital, the vast majority of my patients were less ill than they were damaged—gunshot wounds, car wreck injuries, drownings, accidents.

As I went over Shoshanna's charts, I felt the cold finger of fear tickling my guts, and what I was wondering was, what if by going in to minister to her, I ended up carrying something lethal home to my family? It wasn't a rational fear, but it was there nonetheless, and I was simultaneously gripped by that fear and by guilt for feeling it.

"Has she asked for a chaplain?" I asked Teresa. Maybe I wouldn't have to go in after all.

"No," she said, without looking up from the chart she was working on. "But I think she would welcome a visit from you."

"What's her prognosis?"

"We're trying to keep her alive," Teresa said, and her eyes flashed up to mine, as if to say, "I'm doing my job. Now you do yours."

I nodded. This was the first time Teresa had asked me to visit a patient, and I needed to honor my responsibility to her. Moreover, I had a responsibility to Shoshanna. So I closed the case files, took a deep breath, and opened the glass sliding door into Shoshanna's room.

She was very sick—as sick as any living person I saw that summer, swollen to the point of absurdity, mumbling incoherently. Her eyes bulged as they turned to follow me coming closer to introduce myself, and then, without warning she grasped me and pulled me to her. Never mind my earlier panic; this was the real thing.

It took me a moment to interpret what she was saying, but then all of a sudden, like some new day of Pentecost, I got it.

What she was saying was, "Praise the Lord! Praise the Lord!"

Shoshanna could barely speak, and her tongue was so swollen that it lolled out of her mouth, which is what made her hard to understand, so I had to lean in close and listen carefully. "Praise the Lord," she was saying, over and over again. "I ain't never had no preacher visit me before."

It wasn't healing, although we prayed for that—first in my prayer, then in hers, which was long and mumbled but clearly heartfelt, and went on for five minutes after I had concluded. She still remained in critical condition after my visit and our prayers together. But what had touched her was that my presence represented a relationship with God that had not been cut off—whatever she might have done and been, however she suffered. I was some kind of proof that God still cared for her.

And clearly, she still wanted that relationship as well.

Some of the Psalms of Disorientation are so challenging you will rarely hear them read in Jewish or Christian congregations. The darkness they acknowledge is frightening—too frightening, for many, since they never resolve into new life and health. As Brueggemann notes,

> The use of these "psalms of darkness" may be judged by the world to be *acts of unfaith and failure*, but for the trusting community, their use is *an act of bold faith*, albeit a transformed faith. . . . it insists that the world must be experienced as it is and not in some pretended way. . . . it is bold because it insists that all such experiences of disorder are a proper subject for discourse with God.[12]

These challenging psalms of individual and communal lament, in other words, are normative because they admit life's difficulty and suggest that life, as we live it, good and bad, may all be brought to God in faith that he still hears us.

Let's look at the first portion of Psalm 88, one of the "problem psalms," with Shoshanna's story in mind. Remember her, lying in danger of death, in pain and looking grotesquely distorted because of her illnesses, and imagine her—or someone like her—calling out to God. As we'll see in the verses that follow, although that plea does not dispel the darkness and the psalm ends as it begins, in despair, it does in some way mitigate that darkness by providing an ear that hears these words of complaint. God is present and listening, even though God has not moved to save the pleader, and (as Anderson and Bishop note) the speaker does not, as in most psalms, express a belief that God will intervene:[13]

> O LORD, God of my salvation,
>   when, at night, I cry out in your presence,
> let my prayer come before you;
>   incline your ear to my cry.
>
> For my soul is full of troubles,
>   and my life draws near to Sheol.

I am counted among those who go down to the Pit;
    I am like those who have no help,
like those forsaken among the dead,
    like the slain that lie in the grave,
like those whom you remember no more,
    for they are cut off from your hand.
You have put me in the depths of the Pit,
    in the regions dark and deep.
Your wrath lies heavy upon me,
    and you overwhelm me with all your waves. . . .

You have caused my companions to shun me;
    you have made me a thing of horror to them.
I am shut in so that I cannot escape;
    my eye grows dim through sorrow.
Every day I call on you, O LORD;
    I spread out my hands to you.

(Ps. 88:1–9)

Moralists might have condemned Shoshanna as a sinner who had betrayed her faith; I was moved beyond belief by my time with her, and by my later visits. If I had been Shoshanna, suffering and alone, again, would I have been so faithful to the notion of divine relationship? Would I have drawn comfort from the mere fact that God continued to love and be near me if God didn't fix me up and turn me loose? Or would I have turned my face to the wall, maybe even cursed the chaplain who represented God?

Being faithful in good times is no real measure of religious belief; rather, the real measure is faithfulness in dark times, when God does not move heaven and earth, when, as with the rabbis in Auschwitz, faith has not been rewarded and prayers remain unanswered (or as was recently revealed of Mother Teresa, that throughout her monumental ministry, she prayed but could not feel God's comforting presence). F. W. Dobbs-Allsopp says, in writing about the form and function of the Hebrew book of Lamentations, such laments are a witness to the greatest fidelity to God: "They stake all on God, even in times of deepest despair, when all evidence speaks against God's continuing relevance."[14] Like Kierkegaard's narrator, I can really do nothing but marvel at Shoshanna, shunned, broken, and all but dead, yet continuing to hold onto her faith in and relationship to God.

Shoshanna's story also brings to mind that of Job, tested by the permission of God, who said that even in the midst of his suffering, Job would not abandon his faith. We remember the core of the story easily enough. Satan, the Adversary, hears God say, "Did you notice my servant Job? There is no one on earth like him; a man of perfect integrity, who fears God and avoids evil."[15]

"Sure he does," Satan says. "Who wouldn't? You take such good care of him, fence him in from harm on every side. But what if things were to go bad for him? Then what would he do?"

Well, what Job does when God allows his affliction is three things: he first tells his wife that they must accept bad as well as good from God; for most of the rest of the book, he sits listening to and disputing with the pious and well-meaning friends who want to convince him that he must have done something wrong to merit such punishment; and in language and imagery that stuns us if all we know is "the patience of Job," he takes God to task for what seems to him an awful lot like arbitrary pain and suffering—or like a failure of justice.

Job is one of the great narrative poems in any language as well as perhaps the great dramatic work on God and suffering, and as Rabbi Kushner has pointed out, it revolves around the confluence of three stories, all of which are assumed to be true (but cannot be, if Job's individual story is to have any meaning):

1. God is all-powerful and responsible for everything that happens on earth;
2. God is just and fair, so people get only what their actions deserve; and
3. Job is a good man, as God told the Adversary in the prologue.[16]

Like the Jews in Auschwitz who asked hard questions about God, Job responds to his friends' suggestions that he has somehow offended God by assuring them he has not, and like those in the concentration camp, after a litany of lament, he holds a trial for God:

> Surely one does not turn against the needy,
>   when in disaster they cry for help.
> Did I not weep for those whose day was hard?
> Was not my soul grieved for the poor?
> But when I looked for good, evil came;
> and when I waited for light, darkness came.
>   (Job 30:24–26)

At last, Job does what in the ancient world would be like hiring a high-priced legal eagle and issuing a subpoena: he takes an oath that he is innocent of any wrongdoing. What this means is that God, as accuser, either has to show up and produce the evidence of his evil, or drop the charges. Job asks God for answers, and unlike most of us, in this story Job gets them, a flood of them, although they are couched in the form of rhetorical questions like these:

> Where were you when I laid the foundation of the earth?
>   Tell me, if you have understanding.
> Who determined its measurements—surely you know!
>   Or who stretched the line upon it?
> On what were its bases sunk,
>   or who laid its cornerstone
> when the morning stars sang together
>   and all the heavenly beings shouted for joy?
>   (Job 38:4–7)

Although the traditional pious reading of Job that usually considers only the prologue, God's monologue, and the epilogue (where Job is rewarded and God affirms his virtue) suggests simply that Job is patient and God is compassionate, translator and scholar Marvin Pope points out that this reading ignores nine-tenths of the book. In the dialogue between the friends and Job that makes up the majority of the book of Job, Job frankly questions God's justice. In fact, as Pope notes, "the vehement protests of the supposedly patient Job would surprise and even shock any who expect to find the traditional patient and pious sufferer throughout."[17]

People have sometimes supposed that the book of Job represents our definitive answer to the question "Why?" Job is rewarded for his faithfulness, they say, or Job realizes that he shouldn't ask God to justify himself. The truth is, believing that the book of Job provides a clear answer about suffering is about as smart as believing that Job's know-it-all friends actually know anything. As Pope notes, the book does just the opposite: it "fails to give a clear and definitive answer" to the problem of evil and suffering, and God's complete evasion of Job's oath challenge is the writer's "oblique way of admitting that there is no satisfactory answer available to man apart from faith."[18]

I know it's a long way from "the book of Job is the answer to suffering and death" to "the book of Job says there is no answer," but I'm going to put my weight down on this interpretation because it seems to be most useful for us in our own suffering. The book of Job works very much like those psalms of reorientation; Job loses everything, he is broken, hurt, and confused, and then he finds a new way of seeing God, the world, and himself that makes sense—better sense, in fact, than anything he had believed before or that his friends had tried to sell him, although that sense does not come without pain, experience, growth.

So I agree with translator Stephen Mitchell, who says that the theme of the book of Job is actually spiritual transformation, not the meaning of suffering or the role of God within it.[19] Job begins as someone a lot like us; he has God in a box, he has never had any reason to question his thinking, and it isn't until grief and loss crack his story open that he has to scramble for a new set of meanings. He tries to put God back in a box, and it can't be done—but when God is revealed to him, a rush of word and image that is a true *theophany*, a revelation of God in the world, Job is transformed.

His silence in the face of this revelation is not some mealy-mouthed "I better keep quiet"; it is, as Mitchell and others have noted, a surrender to God in faith. Job has revised all of his stories about God; he has, as J. H. Wheaton says, given up a faith in "the formulas of a well-drilled piety" for "faith without dishonesty or illusion, faith that wins in the teeth of senseless chaos."[20]

"This is the world you inhabit," God is essentially telling Job in the great monologue from out of the whirlwind. "It is a place of chaos and suffering. But it is the only world you have. And I am here. I will not desert you." It is not, perhaps, the answer we want, the story we want to tell, but it is a reaffirmation that even in the most horrible of times, even when we cannot imagine how, God is good and faithful.

Thomas Merton said something that has gotten me through some very dark times, through panic and pain and loss. "All desires but one can fail," he wrote. "The only desire that is infallibly fulfilled is the desire to be loved by God."[21] Let me repeat that so it sticks: *All desires but one can fail, and that is the desire to be loved by God.* God is faithful forever. Furthermore, Job's choice of relationship—to dialogue with God, rather than to turn away, or to deny God, is a vital faithfulness of his own that leads to his transformation.

As my friend Charlie Cook says, "That'll preach."

Moreover, like the process story of God we examined in chapter 1, while we lose something if we give up our notion of God as some kind of cosmic Coke machine we can put quarters in, push a button, and get the outcome of our choice, we receive something new and powerful in the idea of the presence of God working alongside us. As Kushner writes, the end of the book of Job delivers a new hope to us: that "we will turn to God, not to be judged or forgiven, not to be rewarded or punished, but to be strengthened and comforted."[22]

The Jewish tradition teaches us that grief is a normative experience worth sitting with, as Job and his friends do for the seven days that they sit in silence. It teaches us that it is OK to ask questions, to contest with God in difficult times, as both Abraham and Job do without losing their faith in the God with whom they disagree or by whom they feel hurt. One of the reasons that many Christians are so shattered by grief and suffering is that they have no place in their stories for God when things remain undone, when suffering is unmitigated, when death comes (as it always does).

Life contains suffering. (The first of Buddhism's Four Noble Truths actually reads, "Life *is* suffering.") In the psalms, the darkness is not always relieved by light. In Job, natural disasters, personal affliction, and triumphant enemies rob Job of almost everything except that life of suffering.

But what the Hebrew books of Psalms, Job, and Lamentations can give us is a faith story in which one can believe in God—and in which God can still be faithful to those He loves—despite the fact that we do not understand why our lives or the lives of those we love continue to be touched by suffering. It offers a model of individual and communal grief in which we can ask God questions, and not feel guilty or unfaithful for doing so. As Brueggemann points out about the Psalms of Disorientation, in them "being confident of God does not lead to passive acceptance."[23] It's OK to wrestle with God, to ask hard questions, to wonder why things aren't different.

These Jewish Scriptures also offer us a story of faithfulness that we can cling to in those hard times despite the prevailing pull of so many of our stories toward good news and progress. A God who does not end our suffering, but who is aware of us, loves us, and is faithful to us, may for many people be more desirable than a God we control by our wishes, whims, and supposedly pious behavior.

Chapter Four

"Jesus Will Come on Time"

Stories of Grief from the Christian Testament

> For I am convinced that neither death, nor life, nor angels, nor rulers, nor things present, nor things to come, nor powers, nor height, nor depth, nor anything else in all creation, will be able to separate us from the love of God in Christ Jesus our Lord.
>
> Rom. 8:38–39

"Jesus Raised Lazarus"

When we come to the Christian Testament, the stories of grief continue, but with some important differences from the grief tales of the Hebrew Bible. First, in the Gospels and the books that expound upon the life of Jesus, we are offered the example of a savior who actually defeated death and returned to walk the earth, albeit it in a new and transformed way. With few exceptions (such as the boy that the prophet Elijah raises from the dead in 1 Kgs. 17), people who die in the Hebrew Testament generally have the decency to stay dead. But in the Gospels and stories of the early church, we discover people popping out of the grave and back to life with some regularity as Jesus and his followers travel about performing signs and wonders pointing toward the coming reign of God.

One might imagine that Jesus came to inaugurate a paradigm shift about life and death, and one would be right, but it might also

be easy to misunderstand this paradigm shift. *Right to life* is a political slogan, not a theological one, and believing that Jesus makes
it possible for the dead to walk again in this life is to conflate the
Christian teachings about spiritual life in Christ with the Hebrew
Scriptures' concern with the physical world and this life.

Jesus and his followers did not raise all the dead any more than
they healed all the sick, so clearly some new reality where we
might expect the dead to rise again is more an image out of *Dawn
of the Dead* than a theological truth. The signs and symbols of
Jesus' work did point toward the inauguration of a new way of living, dying, and being—

But, as we said, it would be easy to misunderstand this new way.

It had been, without a doubt, my hardest night on call to date;
later that week, my peers would vote it the worst on-call of the
summer, which dubious prize was, at least, confirmation of my
suspicions. My evening had begun with the dead twins I baptized
at Seton Northwest; from there, I had been called back to Brackenridge to secure a mother's permission to take her adult son,
dying of massive systems failure in the ICU downstairs, off life
support. In the middle of that negotiation, I was paged again, by
the ER charge nurse of Children's Hospital, fortunately (or unfortunately) just a couple of halls away.

As the nurse told me "They're asking for you right now," I
could hear somebody (or somebodies) speaking loudly in Spanish
behind her.

So the night just got better. While I have taken Spanish, it has
never really taken to me. I can read it, some, and ask some useful
questions in the present tense, but I cannot really conduct a conversation, and whenever it had come down to theological drama
over Hispanic trauma during the summer, I had put in a call to
Pablo or another Spanish-speaking chaplain.

But all the same, I excused myself with the permissions forms,
handed them to the ICU doctor who had asked me to get them,
then sprinted down the hall and into the back entrance of the
Children's ER, brightly lit and colored. With a tilt of her head, the
charge nurse directed me back into the examination bays.

A Hispanic man and woman, husband and wife, stood outside an emergency bay where a little girl about my son Chandler's age lay motionless and intubated. So I knew it was bad, and it didn't get better as the three doctors who were huddled together turned to me and welcomed me into the conference.

The girl, Madeline, was nine years old; she had an inoperable brain tumor; the tumor had grown so large in the past few months that it was shutting off her body's functions one by one, breathing being the most immediate of those functions.

"She stopped breathing on the way in," the short doctor told me. "So the EMS tech intubated her." She was solemn. "I wish he hadn't done that."

"She's not going to live through this," the tall doctor explained.

"She should have been allowed to die in the ambulance," the third doctor said crossly. "There is absolutely no chance that she will ever breathe for herself."

"Okay," I said, quietly, nodding at the parents and at the Hispanic man and woman standing next to them. "Do they know?"

"Ask *her*," said doctor number three, the surly one, indicating the other Hispanic woman standing nearby.

That's where things got complicated. The woman pulled me out of the conclave and introduced herself as the ER social worker. "That's their pastor," she said, indicating the other man.

"Do they know?" I repeated.

She shook her head, her lips grimly together. "I did not want to translate for the doctors," she said, and her face was stricken. "It's too horrible. And he"—their pastor—"has a daughter just the same age. He does not want to tell them either."

I patted her shoulder and tried to seem steadier than I felt; I too had a child the same age. "I'm going to need you to translate for us," I said, putting my hand on her shoulder. "I'm sorry. I can't answer their questions, but the doctors can."

She took a deep breath and nodded.

I turned to the father and mother and held out my hand, which he shook. "Soy capellán," I told them. *I am the chaplain.* Then I said something intended to be, "We must talk with the doctors now."

I must have gotten pretty close. The father looked me in the eye, then slowly nodded as well.

We all—eight of us, now—crowded into an empty examination room nearby, and the short doctor, Dr. Monroe, told the parents sentence by sentence that their daughter was going to die.

She told them that the tumor, which they knew had been growing bigger and bigger, was starting to shut down all the brain functions that kept Madeline alive. Now it had shut down her breathing function, although later it would be other things. Everything.

She told them that their daughter could not breathe now without the help of machines.

She told them that they could not keep her on the machines, that it wouldn't be right.

She told them that they would have to let her go.

And at last, with all the news translated, the husband looked at me and began to give his testimony. In Spanish, of course, although I found I understood an awful lot—too much, in fact—of what he was saying.

The gist of it was this: My name is Miguel Ruiz, he said. I am a Christian. I believe in Jesus Christ. And I believe that Jesus will heal my daughter.

The translator told the doctors what Miguel had said.

And all three of them just looked at me, as if to say, OK, do something.

And then it got better. "Jesus levante Lazaro," he said. *Jesus raised Lazarus.* "And he will raise Madeline, even if she dies. Con respeto," he said, and he bowed to the doctors. *With respect.* "I hear what you are saying."

He smiled, sadly, wisely, as though he bore some secret understanding none of us possessed.

"But Jesus will come on time."

Well, his pastor was pleased with him, I'll tell you that much. He smiled big. Someone, at least, had been listening to his sermons.

But the doctors impressed me. They were patient, they treated Miguel and his beliefs with respect, and at the same time, they told him, firmly, that he needed to make some medical decisions. It was what, in our patient charting, was meant when we chaplains used to check the outcome box "Encouraged mature outlook."

If Jesus chose to raise Madeline from the dead, fine and dandy. These doctors would line up to shake his hand. But the medical reality was this—Madeline was dying, and her parents had to prepare themselves for that reality and make some choices around it.

Jesus will come on time.

What do we do with this? I've been encouraging you to lean in the direction of hope. And certainly the Christian story is about hope in the face of death; Søren Kierkegaard once wrote that "in the Christian understanding of it death itself is a transition into life," and I hold that as an article of faith.[1]

So what does the Christian Testament—and in particular the life of Jesus, our embodiment of God's will and way—have to teach us about grief and suffering, about the presence of death?

This story about Madeline and her family could teach us some negative things about faith, of course, at the very least that faith does not insulate us from disaster, nor does it rescue us from the necessity of painful choices. In fact, as Barbara Brown Taylor points out, the life of Jesus—so far as we know, the only perfect human life on record, lived totally in accord with God's desires—is irrefutable proof that "goodness is no protection from pain . . . Jesus was as good as good gets, and still he suffered pain—all kinds of pain."[2] Jesus knew spiritual pain, emotional pain, and physical pain, pain in his own person, and pain for those who suffered around him.

But in many ways, I think Miguel starts us in the right place. The raising of Lazarus is a central moment in the story of Jesus; it's the one that shows him displaying very human emotions—anger, sadness, grief. It's here that Jesus wept.

And it's here that we ought to begin—with the first people who believed that Jesus would, indeed, come on time.

> Now a certain man was ill, Lazarus of Bethany, the village of Mary and her sister Martha. Mary was the one who anointed the Lord with perfume and wiped his feet with her hair; her brother Lazarus was ill. So the sisters sent a message to Jesus,

"Lord, he whom you love is ill." But when Jesus heard it, he said, "This illness does not lead to death; rather it is for God's glory, so that the Son of God may be glorified through it." Accordingly, though Jesus loved Martha and her sister and Lazarus, after having heard that Lazarus was ill, he stayed two days longer in the place where he was.

Then after this he said to the disciples, "Let us go to Judea again." (John 11:1–7)

The Gospel of John differs from the other canonical Gospels in some important ways—it has very few signs or miracles compared to the Synoptic Gospels, it reorients teaching from the kingdom of God to belief in the person of Jesus, and it has the highest Christology of the four Gospels. Simply put, that means that in John, the balance between God and man that we find in the idea of the incarnation is tilted heavily over toward the God side of the equation; Jesus controls everything in the Gospel up to and including his own crucifixion. So it's no wonder here in the matter of his friend Lazarus, that he seems to know exactly what he is doing, how things are going to play out. Even though his friend is sick, he waits several days to go to him, until he knows that Lazarus is dead. There will be no question about the miracle that is coming; Lazarus will be in the tomb for days and beginning to smell before Jesus arrives.

When he arrives, of course, he finds a community in mourning. The ritualized custom of grieving—of wailing and mourning the newly departed—is well established elsewhere in the Christian Testament. In the Gospel of Mark, for example, Jesus arrives to raise the daughter of Jairus and finds her dead and her family and friends already in mourning:

When they came to the house of the leader of the synagogue, he saw a commotion, people weeping and wailing loudly. When he had entered, he said to them, "Why do you make a commotion and weep? The child is not dead but sleeping." (Mark 5:38–39)

Jesus tells the mourners that it is not the time or place to grieve, and to confirm his words, he takes the girl by the hand and brings her back to life. But there is a time and place for ritualized mourning around the departed, and it is, as the Jews demonstrate, a vital part of the human process of grief. Writer and undertaker Thomas Lynch, who should know some things about ritualized grieving, puts it this way:

> A good funeral . . . serves the living by caring for the dead. It tends to both—the living and the dead—because a death in the family happens to both. A good funeral transports the newly deceased and the newly bereaved to the borders of a changed reality. The dead are disposed of in a way that says they mattered to us, and the living are brought to the edge of a life they will lead without the one who died. We deal with death by dealing with the dead, not just the idea but also the sad and actual fact of the matter—the dead body.[3]

A similar kind of grieving takes place in the Gospel of John around Lazarus's death, a further reminder of the importance of ritual and of real mourning over the departed, which in our culture is sometimes institutionalized to the extent that it seems abstract and impersonal.

Other things than the raising of the dead are going on in this passage (although that would certainly be enough for most folks). The first sister, Martha, comes out to Jesus and tells him that she wishes he had been there earlier, since she knows he could have prevented their brother's death. But, she says, she knows that God will still do anything Jesus asks for.

It's then that Jesus tells her that her brother will rise again, not in the last days, but now. "I am the resurrection and the life," he tells her. "Those who believe in me, even though they die, will live, and everyone who lives and believes in me will never die. Do you believe this?" (John 11:25–26)

It's one of several "Huh?" moments in the Gospel of John. In another, earlier in the book, when he has told a Jewish leader that one must be reborn if he is ever to know God fully, the man can only imagine that possibility literally, and asks, "How can a person go back into his mother's womb?" (John 3:4).

But Martha sees through the eyes of faith, and the difficulties pass over her. In her confession of Jesus, she acknowledges him as the one with power over life and death:

> She said to him, "Yes, Lord, I believe that you are the Messiah, the Son of God, the one coming into the world."
>
> When she had said this, she went back and called her sister Mary, and told her privately, "The Teacher is here and is calling for you." And when she heard it, she got up quickly and went to him. Now Jesus had not yet come to the village, but was still at the place where Martha had met him. The Jews who were with her in the house, consoling her, saw Mary get up quickly and go out. They followed her because they thought that she was going to the tomb to weep there. When Mary came where Jesus was and saw him, she knelt at his feet and said to him, "Lord, if you had been here, my brother would not have died." When Jesus saw her weeping, and the Jews who came with her also weeping, he was greatly disturbed in spirit and deeply moved. He said, "Where have you laid him?" They said to him, "Lord, come and see." Jesus began to weep. (John 11:27–35)

It's Jesus' own grief here, just before he knows he is going to restore Lazarus to life, that strikes us; it's a normative thing, we have said, for people in that culture to be voluble with their grief, although this incident—the raising of Lazarus and Jesus' tears—appears only in the Gospel of John. Even though the author of John is convinced that Jesus has delayed his visit to Bethany for the express purpose of performing this miracle, nonetheless, at the graveside of his friend, he weeps.

As the Incarnate One whom Martha confesses to be God's Chosen, the Messiah, Jesus is our example of God in action. As Thomas Merton puts it, "Jesus is the theology of the Father, revealed to us."[4] Embodied as he is in the shape of a human life, Jesus represents our best chance in the biblical narrative to understand God's desires and actions in the form of a human story, which is the only form we can readily apprehend.

So what are some of the possible stories behind Jesus' grief in this narrative? Rudolf Bultmann argues that these tears are simply a plot device, a trigger that sparks the next action in the story; Jesus' tears have "hardly any other purpose than to provoke the utterance of the Jews," the rebukes of Jesus that immediately follow Jesus' weeping in the narrative.[5] With all respect for Bultmann's monumental scholarship, this is not a very satisfying narrative reading, because it doesn't make for much of a human story. It's as irritating in its own way as all of those moments in the Gospels when Jesus is said to be doing something simply because it fulfills the prophecies about the messiah. Fulfilling prophecies is the business of God, but it is not done by the human person of Jesus, the one with whom we can identify and from whom we can learn.

So let's consider some more human possibilities. First, humans do things because they must. My great fiction-writing teacher, Robert Olen Butler, has always expressed this drive in terms of *yearning*. Characters in stories do what they do—laughing when they're happy, crying when they're sad, turning over tables in the temple when they're outraged or want to make a point—out of some deep yearning. And if we are to regard Jesus—even here in the Gospel of John—as both fully God and fully human, as the creeds say, then there has to be a marriage of these parts.

So first, I'd propose the simplest narrative solution, one that would make E. M. Forster happy: honest grief. Lazarus is a friend whom Jesus loves, someone whose suffering would affect Jesus the human being (even if the God understanding of Jesus knew he was going to bring Lazarus back to life). Because, just as at the end of Job's story, you can restore a character to what he had, but you cannot take away the pain and suffering he has had to endure. And what Jesus' honest and very personal grief might remind us in this story, as my friend and teacher Cynthia Briggs Kittredge reminds us in her study of John, is that weeping as an expression of grief is a natural and necessary response to loss, echoed later in the Gospel when Mary Magdalene weeps at the tomb of Jesus himself.[6]

We might imagine also that this grief is more expansive—a marriage of the God and man persons of Jesus. As he hears the expressed suffering of the mourners, as he reflects on the human condition—since Eden, to struggle, to suffer, to die—Jesus is moved to pity for Lazarus, certainly, but also to compassionate feeling for Mary, for Martha, for the wailing Jews, for all of suffering humanity. In accepting this interpretation, we can imagine our own compassion excited for those outside ourselves, feel our own pity kindled for those who suffer nearby and far away.

One of my favorite understandings of this story is that of Robin Griffith-Jones, who says it is the contrasting responses of Martha and Mary that prompt Jesus' grief. Both lament that Jesus was not there earlier, and believe their brother would still be alive if he had only come. But Martha accepts that God can still move, even at this late date, while Mary cannot see beyond her pain, and Jesus responds to this:

> Jesus is more upset at the tomb of Lazarus than in any other scene of our gospels; when he meets Mary and sees her despair, he weeps. . . . nothing in Jesus' public work reveals God more clearly than this: that he weeps at the death of a friend—and at Mary's despair, who sees no hope in the presence and promise of God.[7]

Hope is a difficult and seemingly perilous thing, so we should not condemn Mary in her hopelessness. We ourselves have probably been guilty of it at one time or another, even in the presence of God, because hope requires us to look beyond our present circumstances and the difficulties of the moment and to put our trust in something we can neither see nor control. Thomas Merton wrote that, for him, this trust became possible if he let "faith elevate, heal, and transform the light of my mind" and if he also exercised his freedom of will to act in support of that faith.[8] This, as we will see, is a vital part of living in Christian hope.

Jesus in Pain

There is yet another possible reading of this story, though, again imagining the marriage of Jesus' God and man natures. In this section of the Gospel of John, we are given to understand that when Jesus raises Lazarus from the dead, it will be the final straw for the Jewish leaders who have been plotting against him. In a very real narrative sense, Jesus' act of mercy and healing here leads directly to his own agonizing death. Is it possible, then, that when Jesus weeps he is weeping for Lazarus, weeping for the sisters, weeping for suffering humanity—and weeping for himself and the painful future that must come from his doing what he must?

This possibility suggests that we should look at the moment of Jesus' own great experience of personal grief, his dark night of the soul, to see how he deals with anguish. In each of the Synoptic Gospels (and in a similar but very short parallel section in John), just before his arrest, show trial, and crucifixion, Jesus goes out across the valley to a place called Gethsemane, where he begins to wrestle with his feelings about what is about to happen to him. The version in Mark tells us, "Then he took Peter and James and John with him. And he began to feel terror and anguish. And he said to them, 'My soul is sorrowful to the point of death. Wait here, and stay awake'" (Mark 14:33–34 NJB).

Other translations use slightly different words for the original Greek; the New Revised Standard Version says that Jesus "began to be distressed and agitated," and that he was "deeply grieved, even to death," but it's clear that we are dealing with a serious and startling sadness however we translate it. Jesus is suffering.

How will he deal with it?

Whether we think of Jesus at this point as the Gospel of John's Divine One who is pulling all the strings or as the Gospel of Mark's rabble-rousing rebel doesn't particularly matter. One doesn't have to have knowledge of the future to read the writing on the wall: because of the things that Jesus has done and said, the authorities will come for him, soon, and his fate will be the fate of thousands of other Jews over the years who have antagonized the Roman Empire.

Jesus has, probably since his childhood, seen the bodies hung on crosses along the roads outside Jesusalem, and he knows what is coming: Jesus will be taken, he will be tried, and then, without further ado, he will be crucified, a death intended to strike terror into all who witnessed.

It's no wonder that here, as Jesus stares into the heart of what he knows must happen next, he feels deep sadness, sorrow, or even, as the Greek verb *ademonein* (αδεμονειν) suggests of his emotional state in this passage, terror. Further, all the consolations we might hope for when we experience grief—community, a sense of fellow suffering—are missing. Jesus is alone; his closest friends are unable to stay awake to pray with him—and unable to understand what he is going through in any case.

And so, like many characters in the grief stories we have looked at, he prays. We can tell from his prayer that he clearly has an idea what he would like to happen: "I'd really like for you to take this cup from me," he tells God. *I don't want to be tortured. I don't want to die. So if it's all the same to you, that's what I'm hoping.*

This is a familiar prayer for many of us, even if our circumstances might have been a little different. We've prayed for what we wanted, thought we knew best what would be best for us. *God, if it's all the same to you, please don't let me lose my job. Please don't let my husband leave me. Please don't let my mother die. And, oh yeah, could I please have a million dollars?*

But notice how Jesus' prayer, fraught with emotion as it is, contains one element that we sometimes leave out of our own prayers:

> And going on a little further he threw himself on the ground and prayed that, if it were possible, this hour might pass him by.
>
> "*Abba*, Father!" he said, "For you everything is possible. Take this cup away from me. But let it be as you, not I, would have it." (Mark 14:35–36 NJB)

Jesus asks for what he wants—more, he clearly has a very strong preference. He is distressed, distraught, filled with terror, even, about the fast-approaching future. But nonetheless, he says this: "You know what I want. But what I want most is what you want."

Jesus prays three times in all. He prays hard. The Gospel of Luke's version says that Jesus is in agony, that his sweat falls from him like drops of blood. But at the end of it all, he gets up, he wakes up his sleeping friends (who have been no help at all, although he asked them to watch and pray with him), and he faces the future.

Because his prayer, finally, has not been, "Give me what I want."

It has been, "Align my will to yours; you know best what is best for me. And although it will be hard, I will lean into that will with love and faith, for you are God."

This is a hard lesson, but one very much worth learning, for Jesus teaches us in this story about the importance of setting aside faith in the temporal and physical—none of which is going to help him in this narrative—and trusting that whatever happens to him, God is a God of love and justice, and that, even in the terrifying events that may unfold, redemption and resurrection are—will always be—at work.

Perhaps no one has put this better than Rowan Williams, who writes that

> God's presence to the world is neither menacing nor neutral.
> God identifies with the victims . . . we learn this in the fact
> that the bearer of his grace and power in our history is one
> who can be described as "purely" victim . . . yet because the
> life of God is not a life with worldly limits, worldly con-
> straints on its possibilities, the memory of suffering is . . .
> embedded in an inexhaustible life.[9]

And now, at last, we begin to see how the Christian story of suffering starts to diverge from the stories we discovered in Job or the Psalms—or in many of our own stories of how the world works. Christianity imagines an eschatological hope; perhaps we may suffer now, and perhaps that suffering will not be set right in some fashion in this temporal life, but that does not mean that God is unjust or has withdrawn his love, as it might in those other stories. God is willing, able, and moving the world toward transformation.

The story of Jesus is also, as uncomfortable as it may make us, a story of physical resurrection, of God's power over death revealed. Even though we understand that God may not move in miraculous ways in our own suffering, we need to keep a corner of vision open to that possibility, since Jesus' story leads us there.

It would probably take another book on miracles or philosophies of prayer to come to a satisfactory understanding of this, but the fact remains: sometimes, people do get better. Healing comes—physical healing—where it seems impossible. I'll tell you frankly that in some ways I dealt better with decline as a chaplain than with resurrection, because decline, at least, I could understand. To make room for God moving in the world was sometimes a stretch for me. And yet on more than one occasion that summer, I witnessed miracles.

Toward the end of the summer, the ICU had an unexpected visitor: Emilio Perez. He was greeted on the sixth floor like a rock star, nurses gathering around him, giving him high fives, asking him questions.

Jolynne was charge nurse that afternoon, so I went over to her. "What's the story?"

She smiled. "You're going to love this one, Padre," she said. "That's Perez, the famous Perez. He was in 606 for weeks in a coma." She indicated the room right across from us. "Thrown riding a bull. He was brain dead. We had a couple of ethics consults—most of us wanted to pull the plug." She sighed. "But the family asked us to give it three months."

Three months was a long time in hospital terms. One of my patients, a young woman in a car crash, had been on the sixth floor in a coma for ten weeks by that time, and they were trying to figure out a way to get her into a rehab situation so they could have that bed—also right across from us. But age eighteen—which Perez was when admitted—is different from eighty in medical math, and, at last, the ethics committee agreed to hold off for ninety days.

"He was brain dead," Jolynne said. "We thought he'd never come out of it. But," she shrugged, a tiny smile growing bigger, "he did."

She took a deep breath, shook her head in happy disbelief as she looked at him, a handsome boy smiling and shaking hands with the medical personnel, turned her head back to her charts. "This makes it all worthwhile."

Nurse Sandra came back down the hall and settled at the station. "Perez is here," she told Jolynne, who nodded and smiled back. "He's walking and talking."

"So I guess he really beat the odds," I said, and Sandra held up her finger to shush me.

"There were no odds," she corrected, waving that finger at me. "He was brain dead, and nerve tissue doesn't grow back." She looked down the hall, where he was walking to the far nurses' station. "And now he's all walky-talky."

It was clear from this that Perez was a miracle to these medical workers, and a welcome one. In the midst of inevitable decline, inexorable death, they had won one. Perez gave them hope that others might come back from impossible odds, that their work was not simply about accompanying people into a good death.

Perez was a resurrection story, and although you and I know that this story is singular, that resurrection almost never happens as we might want it to, here it is. Like Jesus on Easter morning—something happened. God moved in some fashion—whether directly, or through the skill of the doctors and the care of the nurses, or through the healing powers of Perez's young body—to make things right, and things were never the same afterward.

I spoke earlier of John Dominic Crossan's notion of "operational belief," the idea that whether you believe the Bible stories literally or figuratively, those beliefs should make a difference in your life. Rowan Williams has written about the resurrection, one of the most contested stories in the Bible, in the same way:

> What is vital to Christian discourse about the resurrection can be stated exclusively in terms of what happens to the minds and hearts of believers when proclamation is made that the victim of the crucifixion is the one through whom God continues to act and speak.[10]

The resurrection story, however we understand it, should make a difference in our lives; we must make room for the ray of hope that this story might give us, even if we understand, rationally, that most of the time, brain tissue doesn't grow back.

And when people are dead, they usually stay dead.

When We All Get to Heaven

I held the award for hardest on-call from my chaplain peers for only a couple of weeks. My friend and fellow chaplain Steve Vittorini was called in on a single case that actually put my multiple cases in the shade for length and difficulty of ministry. Tom Greeley had left his pregnant wife, Jane, for a moment to go to the store. He came back to find her on the floor, her breathing stopped. Although he rushed her to the Seton ER, she had suffered a coronary embolism and they could not revive her.

And although the ER team did an emergency caesarean, they could not save the baby either.

So here's this guy, Tom: one minute he's happily married, with his first kid on the way. The next he is alone in the world, and everything he loves has been taken from him. Steve spent—literally—all night with him, with our friend Heath taking over for him the next morning when our regular work shifts started.

Steve and Heath said that Tom was full of questions—about God, about heaven. Every now and then, he would turn to them and ask them something, trying to understand, hoping for some hope.

It was as if maybe this horror could be borne if he could find hope—even a distant hope—to cling to.

I had a similar case, an eighty-seven-year-old cancer patient named Howard. I went to visit him in Seton Medical Center on-call one night, after he had asked the nurse to find "someone who loves Jesus" that he could talk to. Well, that description fit me, I guess, and I was on call, so that evening I went up to Howard's room, sat down across from him, and we talked about God. What was God like? Did I really think there was a heaven? And was it OK for us to pray that he stayed alive a little longer on Earth?

Maybe he could get a miracle or something. What did I think?

Well, what I thought was that here was a guy who—like Tom, in a slightly different circumstance—was at the end of his rope, and who would cling to that final inch as long as he could—or who would jump to any other rope he thought he might reach. Who am I—or anyone—to judge what Howard, in extremis, was feeling? For those in the last stages of life, or in the deepest stages of desperation, pie in the sky by and by might even come to seem useful—a possibility of hope.

But in the larger sense of the day-to-day, of our understanding of God working in the world at all times, I am with Desmond Tutu, who says, "I am not interested, nobody is interested in postmortem pies. People want their pie here and now."[11] And I am with Jürgen Moltmann, who argues that if our vision of Christian hope is in no more than the resurrection in the last days and eternal life by and by, then it is insufficient for our needs in this life. As he writes, the true subject of Christian eschatology is not really the end of things at all, but rather the "new creation of all things."[12] We must—like Jesus in the Garden of Gethsemane, like Jesus on the cross—be willing to put our faith and our actions behind this work of transformation. It is not enough simply to wait for God to move in some end days—nor is it enough to live in resignation waiting for that day. We will have to join our wills to God, in hope and in action, so that, as Julian of Norwich famously said, "All shall be well, and all shall be well, and all manner of things shall be well." All cannot be well without our active involvement. This faith and hope should, as John Polkinghorne puts it, induce us now to roll up our sleeves and get to work:

> Eschatological hope is that nothing of good will ever be lost in the Lord. That thought in itself is enough to rebut a kind of other worldly piety that neglects the ethical demands of the present. It assures us that our strivings for the attainment of good within the course of present history are never wasted, but will bear everlasting fruit.[13]

Regardless of whether or not we believe that Jesus understood he would be raised from the dead, his faith—and action—are still stunning. It is the difference between thinking, "Maybe that little branch up there will hold my weight," and throwing yourself onto it to dangle high off the ground. Jesus was putting his faith in a Father who would not desert him, and his belief that all suffering will be transformed by that Father into his actions.

Jesus' own experiences of grief can, then—and should—lead us to resolve to walk by faith and hope—and to match our actions to our beliefs. But how can we do that?

When we examine some of our stories about death, we can begin to see how faith and action might come together. So let us turn our attention next to death, and continue to ask how life can emerge from it.

Chapter Five

The Black Book

Stories of Death

To die will be an awfully big adventure.

J. M. Barrie, *Peter Pan*

Don't Fear the Reaper

In each of the hospitals I worked in—and for all I know, in every hospital—there is a notebook, binder, or journal with a very specific function. In Brackenridge, we had a black journal, called "the Black Book," although it was really the Book of the Dead. Whenever a patient died and we were attending, there were certain things we were supposed to do, and one of them was to write the patient's name, time and date of death, and next-of-kin information in the Black Book.

It was Father's Day, a Sunday early in the summer, and I had just finished recording this information on a couple of tough on-call deaths at other hospitals when I returned to the chaplain's office in Brackenridge to eat something before I took a Bible upstairs for Marvella, at what would be our first meeting. I was sitting at a desk eating a sandwich and a bag of chips when I looked up at the shelf above me, and lo, there was the Black Book.

I was curious. I hadn't had to write in this book yet, but I had been working mostly in this hospital for about two weeks, and I wondered how often our patients died.

Simple as that. How many names would I find in the Black Book?

So I took it down and opened it to the latest page with writing—all the other deaths had happened before I came to Brackenridge, and although their deaths must have been shattering to those who loved them, they meant something to me only in the abstract.

But there were two names entered since I had started my chaplaincy.

There was Hans Kupka, a ninety-four-year-old man who had fallen off a ladder repairing his garage door. He had been unconscious when I left the hospital on Friday afternoon; in fact he had been unconscious since he arrived in intensive care earlier in the week. But I had sat and talked with his wife and daughter in the sixth-floor visitors' area, holding the wife's hand while she told me, her eyes gleaming, "I can't believe this is happening. Last week he was on the roof cleaning out the gutters."

He had seemed so vital, so alive then.

And now he was dead.

And there was Verne, the gay street person who had asked me to help him fill out advanced directives because he wanted a simple dignified death.

I hoped they had given it to him, and that now, at last, his soul was at peace.

On the Thursday before, when we had talked, he had been so emaciated that his legs looked like pipe cleaners, and his underwear hung from him like a sagging diaper when he pushed himself out of bed to search for his glasses.

Verne had been my age, Hans twice my age. Two very different lives. Two very different deaths. But all the same, both of them were in the Black Book.

And both of their stories can teach us about death.

Death may be unexpected.

But death is inevitable.

And it is in our approach to death—in the stories we tell about death—that we will find much about life as well. If death often comes without warning and unannounced, it also comes to everyone, and if we are honest and courageous we will see it coming a long way off and make plans on how to deal with death—both our own, and that of those we love.

It was my last on-call night of the summer, which, mercifully, was winding down. I had only a few hours left of my four hundred-hour chaplaincy, and one last night to get through, and it could not have come at a better time. I was exhausted—emotionally, physically, spiritually—from what I had witnessed and what I had tried to do and be for people in the hospital. Again, I wondered how staff chaplains manage to get out of bed every morning; it was all I could do at this late date to go inside the hospital.

It had been a quiet evening at home. My girlfriend, Martha, and I had had dinner, and the evening had gone on, hour after hour, without my beeper going off. And despite all I have said about the way Jesus teaches us to pray about aligning ourselves with God's will, I was lifting up nothing but selfish prayers, although I tried to make them sound unselfish: *Please, please, please don't let anyone die in a Seton hospital tonight. Please keep the roads clear, please protect all mothers in childbirth, please preserve Austin from drug overdose, drowning, or any other calamity.*

I actually fell asleep, all my clothes on, the beeper on the altar beside my bed, thinking I was going to wake up the next morning, yawn, smile, and thank God for a miraculous night without death or trauma.

The beeper went off at 4 a.m. I sprang up, called the number, and got the staff chaplain of Children's Hospital at home, who told me what was up: Four-year-old girl, Marcy McBee, just diagnosed with a tumor in her brain stem. The surgeons would operate at seven, but they didn't think they could get it all.

And the family was—as you would imagine—freaking.

"Get down there," she told me; she had a tendency toward brusqueness at the best of times, and these weren't them. "Get down there right now."

"On my way," I assured her. I ran my hand through my hair, swished some mouthwash, and grabbed my car keys.

Although not, I'll confess it, without a quick gaze heavenward and a few theologically unsound remarks. Perhaps we could be charitable and say that, like Job, I was arguing with God. I was tired, and soul weary, and it showed: "Couldn't let me have just one night without a tragedy, could you? A four-year-old? Are you [bleeping] serious? What is it with you and brain tumors, anyway?"

Oh, but it was serious, all right. Fifteen minutes later, when I got to Marcy's room, I checked with her nurses, who were grave. Nothing like having a four-year-old facing death to give you a sense of gravity.

I looked at her chart. She was thirty-nine inches tall. She weighed thirty-one pounds.

I thought my heart would break right there in the hallway.

Inside her room, Marcy was lying listlessly in bed with a Gund kangaroo and monkey. Her eyes were open, but she had been given some medication, and she was pretty unresponsive.

Marcy's parents, Anne and Tilden, were good country people, trying to be strong but clearly scared out of their minds. The small room was full of family—aunts, cousins, other children, standing in clusters, sitting, many of them weeping.

Marcy would hardly respond to me when I talked to her, when I chucked her chin. "I think she knows something's wrong," her mother said. But she and Tilden talked to me—they lived on a farm in South Texas, this was totally unexpected, they were so glad I was there.

As we talked, I discovered that they were telling themselves familiar stories about suffering.

"I just keep praying that God will take me instead," Anne told me. "She's such a good girl. She never gets into trouble."

I tried to talk her out of that story, to gently suggest that God did not will her daughter's illness, and that deserve had nothing to do with this—and at last, at their request, I gathered everyone together to pray.

In my tradition, we have an understanding that sometimes slips by unexamined, the awareness that prayer reflects (or should, anyway) our actual beliefs. I tried to be pastoral whenever I prayed with people in the hospital—and yet also true to my understanding of God's place in suffering. So I prayed something that could be boiled down to this: *Lord, you know we seek your will. But you know our desire is healing for Marcy. We ask that you give the surgeons skill and wisdom, and that you give Marcy—and all of us—the strength we will need to get through the next few days. Send your spirit to comfort and guide us. We give you thanks for the work you are doing, even though we cannot see yet what that work might be. Thank you for hearing us.*

I have often heard people pray to God for very definite results. I grew up in another tradition very different from the Episcopal story I live inside now, a tradition where you are encouraged to ask God for exactly what you want, and if your faith is strong enough, you will get it. (Unless of course you don't, but then that's usually just a sign that your faith wasn't strong enough, right?) I could have prayed for healing, for complete remission, for a miracle. There were, after all, two or more gathered together, and I think we could have set our mind to it, since we all wanted the same thing: for this beautiful little girl to walk out of the hospital safe and sound.

But it's also true that miracles are miraculous because they happen so rarely, and often they can't be found when you want one. What Marcy and her family needed was not pie in the sky, to return to Desmond Tutu's analogy, but pie on the ground: strength for the journey, a sense of God's presence, my willingness to journey alongside them for my last few days in the hospital.

The surgery that morning was not successful in getting all the malignant growth; in the year and a half since, there have been other surgeries, also unsuccessful. As I write in December of 2007, Marcy is still alive, and her chemotherapy has kept the tumor at bay. She and her family are the only patients I continue to follow from the hospital, and I continue to pray for her, even though death seems less and less a surprising possibility and more and more possible.

At first Marcy's story just looks a mess, a train wreck. How can we hope that this story of the looming death of a child will lead us to some positive theological understanding?

Well, I think one of the solutions is to look at the two elements of death we introduced early in the chapter: Death may be surprising. Sudden.

But it is also inevitable. It comes to everyone, and while our stories like to insist otherwise, we have no control over when it comes, or to whom.

One of the spiritual traditions to which I am strongly drawn is that of the Desert Fathers and Mothers. What most people remember about them these days is that they were spiritual athletes, showboats trying to outdo each other in who could sleep less, who could wear the fewest clothes on the coldest day, who could go longest without eating. It looks, from that angle, like something not that much different from a couple of kids competing to see who can hold her breath longest.

But what makes the desert tradition powerful in my experience is what I sense in Buddhism and other ascetic traditions as well: When you don't let yourself get too attached to the physical, when you are constantly reminding yourself that all you see will one day fade away, it changes your attitude toward this world. Things become less possessions to hold tight lest someone take them away from you and more something loaned to you for a moment's use.

And if we can begin to imagine holding a little less desperately to the things of this world—even to those whom we love—it becomes easier to imagine them as a gift rather than a right, something we are owed.

I did not introduce this idea to Marcy's parents on our first night together—when you have just been shocked with the realization that your beautiful little girl is on the edge of death, that would not be a helpful observation.

When you are still getting accustomed to the idea of death, when it has been shut up out back of the house or hidden under a rug, it's hard not to live in fear, even though, as Barbara Brown Taylor notes, God's voice has never promised freedom from pain; it has only promised freedom from fear, if we're just willing to trust, completely trust.[1]

But where Marcy's parents sit now, on the edge of the possible, perhaps it becomes—if not easier—at least more logical to be grateful for having her at all, for her days of good health and high spirits, for the knowledge that she was never anything more than a temporary gift to them and to this planet, when it comes right down to it.

That was John Claypool's attitude when he came toward the end of the journey with his daughter's illness and death. In the last of the four sermons he preached on his grief, he retold the story of Job, and in doing so, he came to this realization: Everything Job had lost, his possessions and his children, did not really belong to him in the first place. "They were gifts—gifts beyond his deserving, graciously given him by Another. . . . to be angry because a gift has been taken away is to miss the whole point of life." That we have ever had the things we cherish is, Claypool preached, more than we deserve.[2]

Moreover, "true gratitude," as Henri Nouwen put it, "embraces all of life: the good and the bad." For how can we know, he asks, rightly, what healing will always look like?[3] When I prayed for Marcy on that first morning—and when I pray for her now—my hope is still for her physical healing. But who knows what emotional and spiritual healing may come through this long, hard physical illness? Who knows how God may yet be moving and present in the lives of these people whom I have grown to love, even in the worst that we might imagine?

It's also important to remind ourselves that God is not outside of—or somehow alien to—this mammoth undertaking that sorrow and letting go might represent. In another of the sermons he preached about his little girl's illness and death, Claypool said it meant more to him than he could express that God too was a parent who had to give up his child to suffering and death.

And moreover, that God was a cosmic force who had somehow created light out of that darkness, joy out of that suffering.

"This is the bedrock of my own hope," Claypool preached:

> What God could do for his boy in the midst of suffering I dare to believe that God can do for my girl. I am staking my life on the belief that our present calamity will not end in darkness. Laura Lue may suffer, she may even die, but God will bring her through and us also. And out of whatever happens,

God will not be overcome but will somehow turn this evil to good purpose and in it all bring light out of darkness.[4]

And all I can say to that is amen, and amen.

Light out of Darkness

John Irving, in his novel *The World according to Garp*, wrote that all stories, extended long enough, end in death. If death is, then, inevitable, as we have been suggesting, what else can we learn from a story in which we come to accept death as a fellow traveler?

One thing might be our willingness to live with the experience of not-knowing, of living in between, which is often so alien to us; we like to insist that we are (or should be) in control of every moment of our lives. William James, in his *Varieties of Religious Experience*, translated the German concept *Zerrissenheit* as "torn-to-pieces-hood." At some time in our lives—if not before our impending death—we will be in this place of torn-to-pieces-hood we have talked about since our earliest pages, this place where the stories fall apart and where, thus, nothing makes sense any longer. We can resist with all our might, we can clamber and clamor for meaning, or we can accept that some things are beyond our control, that it is the nature of all human lives that they should end. And while we cannot know for certain what is going to happen, we can gather together to support the dying and the bereaved and offer a gospel of hope, as Claypool argued, that God is moving in the midst of suffering.

One of my favorite deaths that summer (and notice what a bizarre and countercultural phrase that seems) was the death of Jaime, a young Hispanic man in the Brackenridge MICU who had, like others that summer, suffered a sudden systems collapse that landed him in the hospital and shortly after, killed him. His family was Catholic, and they were gathered together, twenty or so of them, to see him off. In one of the few times I was asked to crack it open that summer, I turned in my Book of Common Prayer to the prayers for the dying (the liturgy called "Ministration at the Time of Death"). We prayed for the delivery of Jaime's soul, for mercy, for pardon. But we did not pray for a healing miracle. What we were addressing now was the reality: Jaime was dying, and we wanted to accompany him to the edge of that death and send him on his way with prayer.

Finally, I prayed this commendation:

> Depart, O Christian soul, out of this world;
> In the Name of God the Father Almighty, who created you;
> In the Name of Jesus Christ who redeemed you;
> In the Name of the Holy Spirit, who sanctifies you.
> May your rest be this day in peace,
> And your dwelling place in the Paradise of God.[5]

There was some weeping at this—but there was also some nodding, and I saw peace on the faces of all those there. It was tragic, yes, but somehow some meaning had been restored. In fact, I would go so far as to say that Jaime's was a good death, as Thomas Lynch would define it: a death surrounded by "the faces of family and people who care . . . the death of a whole person, not an ailing part," and a death where family and friends could "be present to the glorious and sorrowful mysteries."[6]

And those mysteries included the mystery of hope emerging out of death and suffering.

Another good death was my first code on-call, an African American man named Marcus, who had lived seven years with a new heart, but would not make eight.

After they had pronounced him dead, I went in with Marcus's wife and sister-in-law. We gathered close to the bed, holding hands, and I laid my hand on Marcus's shoulder. We prayed a more informal prayer for the dead than I would later pray for Jaime—a Baptist prayer, if you will. I prayed a lot of Baptist prayers, extemporaneous and seeking the movement of the Spirit, that summer. Then after we prayed, Marcus's wife let go our hands and stepped forward to lay her hand on his face.

"Thank you, Lord," she said. "Thank you, Lord."

Maybe I had a quizzical expression on my face, because in the hallway, she took my arm as we walked. "Greg, I had seven years with Marcus that we didn't expect. That heart transplant kept him alive. Those years were a gift, pure and simple. I can be grateful for that, no matter how they ended."

Then she nodded to herself. "I *am* grateful for that."

Maybe she thought I wouldn't understand it, but believe me, I do. For several years now I have felt that life—whatever it holds, including suffering and death—is a gift. You have heard some of my own story in these pages, may know some of it from other writing I've done, but essentially it boils down to this: from the time I was a teenager until I was thirty-six, I suffered from low-grade chronic depression, what doctors typically diagnose as dysthymia. It was not originally life-threatening, but it did make me walk around in a fog thinking that life was hardly worth living. Then, after the birth of my son Chandler in 1997, insomnia and unresolved personal issues pushed me into deep, life-threatening depression.

Part of me is still amazed that I am alive today. I was at the edge of death on several occasions, and when I seriously considered suicide, it was not for the dramatic value, not a cry for help, not a call for attention. On the occasions I sat (or stood) beside the abyss and the chemicals in my brain were screaming "Do it!" all I wanted was to end the pain.

I wanted to be dead.

This is a final, sad story of death; I fear that there are too many people who are hoping to be dead, whether it comes quickly or eventually. We all know people who are killing themselves—and who know that they are killing themselves—with their lifestyle choices. We all know (or know of) people who are alone, people who are chronically ill, people who are in pain. When I think of lives I would not want to live, I think particularly of Antonio, who I met my first week in Brackenridge after he got drunk, rolled his boss's truck, and ended up on the sixth floor a paraplegic, paralyzed from the neck down for the rest of his life.

But, somehow, Antonio had hope—he loved his family, he wanted to be alive for his daughters, and he had faith that shaped his life and continued to give it meaning, even in that inert body. I loved my visits with Antonio, and wished I could spread his hope throughout the hospital.

Because in many of the rooms I visited, even when the diagnoses were not fatal, I met with nothing but despair. And I understood that as well, since for so many years I felt nothing but despair myself. The virtue of suicide, if there was one, was that at least the suffering would be over.

But you also know, since I am typing these words now, that while I may have stood at the edge of the precipice, looked into it, even stuck a foot out there and waved it around deciding, I did not step in.

Sometimes that decision not to jump broke my heart, because I could not imagine going on in such pain, causing the people I loved such pain, for I was impossible to live with.

But I didn't jump—or step in front of a truck. Or take a bottle full of sleeping pills. Or crash into a bridge abutment. Without hope, I nonetheless hoped for something to change.

And I didn't die.

In fact, like the marvelous Perez, in the summer of 2003 I experienced what I can only think of as a resurrection. I went off the medication that had kept me alive (not something you should do without consulting your doctor, I note), and on my drive to Ghost Ranch to work on a novel, I began to feel something again, something good after years of feeling nothing but bad.

What I felt, I suddenly realized, was *joy*—joy in the roadside flowers, joy in the colors of the mesas, joy in the expansive blue sky. I was overjoyed to be alive.

And that joy, in large measure, was a direct response to the darkness I had long found myself in. Who'd have thought that anything good could come out of my calamitous life?

But it did. It has. And I am grateful beyond words, although words are all I have. Permit me to crib from myself, because I don't think I have said this better than the way I wrote it several years ago in a book of spiritual autobiography: "I really think of my life now as a gift. That it doesn't belong to me anymore. And so I want to give it serving other people."[7]

For an epigraph to that book, I had used the old Spanish saying "God writes with crooked lines," and my life, suffering, and near death have only confirmed me in that understanding. I can't claim that I have lived a perfect or even very pleasant life—I would dearly love to have been a good husband to at least one of my wives, truly wish I had been able to make healthy decisions in my life and work during the time I was depressed. But would I change my life if I could somehow wave a magic wand?

Not a chance. I am who I am because of that calamitous life, just as you are who you are in large part because of the tumbles and tunnels along your own path. My authentic faith, my joyful life, and the vocations of teaching, writing, preaching, and speaking that I pursue in the world have all grown out of my facing death, enduring suffering, and giving up control of my life to trust God. The gift of my life is my whole life, then, good and bad, light and dark, and what has emerged from it is not only a genuine sympathy for those who suffer, because I have been there, but an understanding of how good can come from that suffering if we are only willing to let it emerge.

I read a lot of Thomas Merton when I was sick, and here are two more of the sentences that led me into a new story of life, death, and God: "Better than hoping for anything from the Lord, besides his love, let us place all our hope in His love itself. This hope is as sure as God Himself."[8]

So here is the ultimate goal of our stories of death: hope. Not a story of bargaining with God for special favors, exemptions, longer life. Not a story about how we shouldn't have to face suffering and death in our own persons or in those we love because we're rich, faithful to God, faithful to medical science, faithful to the American Way. No—we live faithfully, by which I mean we seek God's will in our lives and movement in the world, and because of that, we live in hope, grateful for whatever life gives us. Jürgen Moltmann, who perhaps more than any other contemporary theologian has parked his car in the garage of faithful hope, wrote that bearing authentic faith "means being freed from anxiety for trust, being born again to a living hope, loving life without reserve."[9]

I know I speak for myself and I hope I speak for you when I ask, doesn't Moltmann's authentic faith sound better than living in fear, living in despair, or living in frustration? Hope in God's purpose and love for the gift of life, with all its ups and downs, seems like a powerful and appropriate response to the presence of suffering in this world and to the certainty of death.

And I can tell you as someone who has both observed and known suffering, hope will make the life you live until that death more fulfilling and more joyful than you can possibly imagine.

"Facing Reality"

The Archetypal Story and the Shape of Grief

All sorrows can be borne if you put them into a story or tell a story about them.

Isak Dinesen

The One Story about Suffering

A little more than 2,500 years ago, a baby boy was born to the royal family. Wise men and sages predicted that he would become one of two things—a king or a prophet. The baby's father, anxious for the succession, was horrified. He decided to sequester the boy, keep him away from religious teachings, shield him from suffering, so that he would never be tempted to fulfill the destiny of religious teacher.

And so, for some years, the prince grew, happy from day to day, living a life without conflict, without fear. He married, and found bliss in his life with his new bride.

But the gods were not content for the prince to continue on in his blindness. One day, despite the best plans of his father, as he was riding in his chariot from one palace to another, the prince saw an old man beside the road, his hair frizzled and white, his face wrinkled and worn, his back bent, his steps unsteady and painful.

"What on earth has happened to that man?" the prince asked the driver of his chariot. He was shaken to the core.

"That is an old man," the driver said, and innocently continued, "All of us will look like that some day."

Although the prince would see other sights that would jar his reality and shake his story—sickness, a corpse—this was the moment when he realized that his life was going to change. Life could not go on the way it always had, if this was where he was going to end up. Joseph Campbell said that such moments in all our lives (for they do come for all of us when we are shaken out of our ordinary lives) signify "that destiny has summoned the hero and transferred his spiritual center of gravity to a zone unknown."[1] All of us face a moment in our lives (and often many moments) that challenges our center of gravity, that wants to shift it from a self-serving story to one that will mean something in a larger context.

The prince in our story, as you probably know, was Siddhartha Gautama; we know him today as the Buddha, for after leaving the settled life of ease and stasis he had lived for so long, he wrestled with suffering, learned about pain and deprivation, and reached enlightenment. Today, he is remembered as one of the world's great spiritual teachers, his wisdom on compassion and living mindfully embraced by Christians and Jews as well as Buddhists.

And this wisdom all came because he came face to face with suffering.

Ignorance, the old saw says, is bliss. But life rarely permits us to live in ignorance, nor should it. "All human unhappiness comes from not facing reality squarely, exactly as it is," the Buddha once said, and in our own quest for a story that will allow us to face reality squarely, we have one last stop to make.

The Gautama Buddha's story is that of a single human life; as such, it is distinctive. But in its outlines, it is also universal. As an archetypal story, like the lives of Moses, Jesus, the apostle Paul, Martin Luther King, Mother Teresa, and so many literary heroes I can't possibly number them, it shares common narrative features, characters, themes. In that commonality, we can also find ourselves and our own distinctive stories reflected in a way that will allow us to face sorrow, disappointment, loss, and even death with the knowledge that they are a natural and necessary part of this great pattern and not to be feared.

For on the other side of pain, suffering, and even death, this archetypal story insists that there is hope and connection and the opportunity to be our truest, best selves, the people whom God intends us to be.

Joseph Campbell was a professor of mythology who taught for almost forty years at Sarah Lawrence College and longer in the larger world through his lectures, television appearances, and books. He is best known for his work concerning the archetypal hero's journey, a singular narrative pattern he uncovered from his ethnographic research into hero and creation myths from cultures around the world. According to Campbell, cultures across the globe, from Laplanders to Aborigines, from ancient Celts to Native Americans, have told (and continue to tell) a story with a single shape, an archetypal pattern that is populated by distinctive individuals.

In its basic form, the hero's journey goes like this: a person living her normal life in the ordinary world receives a call to adventure. She can accept that call and follow where it leads, or she might (as we often do) refuse it and try to continue on in her ordinary life. In any case, she chooses or is forced into a path that takes her out of her ordinary life and crosses a threshold into a world of adventure. There, she often descends into the belly of the whale, as in the story of the Hebrew prophet Jonah, where she is tested.

On her new path, she encounters challenges and discovers allies and enemies. At last she faces an ordeal that tests her newfound heroism and confirms her on the path she has taken. Typically she then receives or retrieves a boon, a gift (tangible or metaphysical) that she will take back to her community. Then she begins her journey home, although it is typically interrupted by one final challenge, an experience of death and rebirth (actual or metaphorical) that is instrumental to her final return to the community with the life-giving boon.[2]

If we consider how this pattern can be viewed as more than an anthropological curiosity or a narrative structure—that is, if we use it, as we have been using all these stories, to discover what they might teach us about our lives—we discover some important things. For instance, we should expect to be put in a place of cognitive dissonance, a place where the old ways no longer work, at least once in our life. And our response to that call to adventure, of course, may be to plant our heads firmly in the sand and hope that it will go away. But if we step out in faith onto the path, although difficulty most assuredly awaits us, we will also find our salvation in the surest and broadest sense. Augustine and the Celtic theologian he branded a heretic, Pelagius, both agreed on one element of our relationship with God: that at birth, we are imprinted with the image of God. How we lose that image and how we might recover it—that they disagreed on. But they and many other theologians have agreed that returning to our truest self, the one created in the image of God, is what salvation is. And setting out on the path of adventure is our route to being the person that God has planned for us to become.

I have talked often in these pages about Marvella, one of my favorite patients and one of my longest-running chaplaincy cases. I'd like to take her stay in the hospital as a retelling of the archetypal hero's journey so that we might discover how this pattern can inform our individual stories.

Let's begin with the ordinary world. That world for Marvella was Brownwood, Texas, where, as you remember, she was a church organist who loved her work. The call to adventure that rocked her world was her first hospitalization, although in a sense she believed that was a temporary aberration, that soon she would be back home playing for the children's choir. She was forced to cross the threshold between worlds when she caught that opportunistic infection in the hospital; she was very sick, and then the doctors discovered that it had incapacitated her kidneys.

When I first met her, she was dealing with pain and sickness—she had gone from her sunlit world into the belly of the beast. And it didn't get better from there, although she had allies along her path. Her sister Ora was beside her every step of the way; her medical team worked alongside her; I was there for spiritual encouragement and support.

It actually got worse. When her kidneys failed, there was only one choice for her—she would have to undergo dialysis. And if her kidney function was gone, she would have to face a lifetime of it. The day she went in for her first dialysis treatment was the beginning of her ordeal. When I saw her after her treatment, she was still in the middle of that ordeal, struggling. She had tears in her eyes as she said, "Greg, it hurt. So bad. I don't ever want to do that again."

But if she was going to stay alive, she would have to do it again, and again, and somewhere in there, something happened that I only witnessed from outside: her faith, which had been transactional and predicated on a belief in reward and punishment, was shaken, stirred, and poured out again in a new shape, a shape of quiet acceptance and a genuine faith that God had a purpose, even though she couldn't see it from where she lay. I had shared with her earlier that summer one of my favorite sayings of H. Richard Niebuhr, that God is always faithful even when we can't discern the manner of that faithfulness. And now, I was watching her live into that belief.

So she emerged from her ordeal, although she was not well, for she was still too sick to leave the hospital, and her kidneys were only functioning at about 6 percent of their capacity. But she had proven herself as a hero of faith, and had gathered a boon of acceptance and hope that she could share with others. Often in the archetypal hero's journey, the boon or reward the hero gains is intangible, if still vital to the survival of the community: a new way of seeing the world, a new understanding of the Divine. And that was what Marvella had, to the consternation of Ora, who still thought that her sister must have done something wrong for God to strike her down like that.

Well, if she had, then suddenly she must have done something very right, because here's the thing that makes this story so perfect: Marvella was sick, so sick that she couldn't leave the hospital. She was walking in the valley of the shadow of death.

Then one afternoon her nurse came up to me as I was about to enter Marvella's room and pulled me aside. "They're working," she said.

"What?" I looked around for painters or some hospital staff somewhere.

"Marvella's kidneys. They've come back online. We stopped her dialysis." She looked at me as though I might be able to explain this. I couldn't; as I said, I still find it easier to explain suffering than miraculous healing, even with my belief in a resurrecting God.

"Wow," I said. "She must be thrilled."

And indeed she was—who wouldn't be thrilled with a resurrection? But it was a quiet thrill. God had known what he was doing all along—and if she had not been healed, even if she had gone to her death, God would still have known what he was doing.

A few days later, Marvella was released from the hospital. I had a short letter from her thanking me for sitting with her, talking to her. She returned to her community with a boon, a story of suffering and healing, a story of hope and faith. And while I haven't talked to her since she left, I'd imagine that she came back home a different person in more ways than one.

When you die and you are reborn, as Jesus knew even before the crucifixion, you become something new, see the world through different eyes.

Lessons from the Archetypal Story

So what can the hero's journey teach us? First, the story suggests to us that change is the constant of the universe. Many of our stories encompass only positive change—bigger house, more money, greater acclaim, better-looking wife. But the omnipresence of change is suggested from the outset of any hero's journey, and we should learn to inhabit a story of our own that makes room for it as well.

I was on a panel at the Austin Film Festival a couple of years ago, and Bill Wittliff (who wrote the screenplays of and produced *Lonesome Dove*, *Legends of the Fall*, and *A Perfect Storm*) had a familiar comment about storytelling that will help us here. "There's really only two stories," he said. "A stranger comes to town, and a man goes on a journey."

The constant of both of those story patterns is disruptive change; when a stranger comes to town she or he brings new ways of doing things, new information, a new story of how to get by in the world. Anyone who meets the stranger will be confronted with change.

The call to adventure in the journey story is also obvious. When we step out our front doors we are exposed to new people, new places, new ideas. This is why I structured my first novel, *Free Bird*, as a journey novel. My narrator, Clay Forester, was (like many of us) so stuck in his ways that nothing was ever going to jar him out of his ordinary world as long as he was in familiar settings. But once I put him on the road, once I took him out of a place where he could order his surroundings, things began to happen to him. Some of those things did not, at first, seem to him to be good things. But they were in the end, because the change that so discomfited him also turned out to be the change that saved him.

Change is an unavoidable part of life. So is suffering, which often results from our inability to accept change. In the crucial moments of the hero's adventure—the belly of the whale, the ordeal, and the death and rebirth—the hero will be tested to her physical, emotional, and spiritual limits. By definition, there is no such thing as a pleasant ordeal. But what the archetypal story teaches us is not to fear suffering. If difficulty, danger, and even death are a natural part of life, then we can accept them as part of the story. To be a hero, Campbell says, means "not withdrawing from the world when you realize how horrible it is, but seeing that this horror is simply the foreground of a wonder. . . . It wouldn't be life if there weren't temporality involved, which is sorrow—loss, loss, loss. You've got to say yes to life and see it as magnificent this way; for this is surely the way God intended it."[3] So when we accept that change and loss are a natural part of the created order, we can live in a different story than when we seek to live in a story that denies them, a story where their appearance strikes us dumb.

The hero's journey also teaches that death and resurrection are a natural part of the cycle of life. Some Christians, following the words of Jesus in John 3, actually describe themselves as being born again. I am drawn to the idea that this born-againness is more about a process, a continued faithfulness on the journey, than it is about a single fateful decision in time. So to the question "Are you born again?" I think, after my initial discomfort, I would have to answer, "I am trying to be."

In some of our stories, the death that precedes rebirth is actual and physical—think of Jesus on the cross and in the tomb; Neo (Keanu Reeves) in the first *Matrix* film when he is killed by Agent Smith; Harold Crick (Will Farrell), my current favorite Christ figure, who in the film *Stranger than Fiction*, thinking he knows full well what awaits him, still rescues a child from being run over by a bus at the cost, he believes, of his own life.

In these cases, we have miraculous interventions—actual bodily resurrections. In other versions of the story, the deaths and resurrections are more symbolic than physical. In them, we walk through the valley of the shadow of death, with darkness pressing in on every hand, but we emerge on the far side, into new life. We were weighed down; we were lost; we were hopeless. But the structure of the archetypal story gives us added hope that death is not the end, that suffering does not have the last word in our own stories, because the possibility of rebirth is inherent in all stories.

And finally the hero myth, like some of the spiritual traditions we have mentioned, reminds us to get over ourselves. We typically think of a hero as a great individual, as someone who performs glorious feats of arms or strength. But Campbell tells us that the hero in the archetypal myth is a hero on behalf of a community, not merely for self. "A hero," he wrote, "is someone who has given his or her life to something bigger than oneself." That hero is on a long journey, with many trials, on the way ultimately to renouncing the self in service of others so that "when we quit thinking primarily about ourselves and our own self-preservation, we undergo a truly heroic transformation of consciousness."[4]

One of the most important parts of my own healing—my emerging from my ordeal, my resurrection into a useful and healthy life, was my willingness, like Marvella, to surrender control of my life to God, and to try to get over myself. In my journal, although this happened before I could will the action required to confirm it, I at least wrote about my obsession with myself and my problems, my inability to get out of my head and see what was going on around me. It was when I gave myself wholly to God and to a faith community that I was permitted to see that God's story of life on earth did not center on me, that my problems, considerable though they might be, did not make much of a splash in the ocean of the world's problems.

If it had been left up to me to recover on my own behalf, I don't think I would be here today. But the hope I was given by my friends Chris, Greg, and others that God was not finished with me yet, that God intended for me to be a part of the healing of the world—well, that was something worth living for.

The hero's journey is generally diagrammed as a circle, with the action beginning at the top of the circle, moving around counterclockwise to the top of the circle, as in the illustration.

A last lesson we might learn from the archetypal story is that in our lives, we may undergo multiple journeys, follow the circle around over and over again, enter into separate adventures with their own disconcerting calls, ordeals, and returns with new wisdom, practice, or faith. To be a knight of faith, as Kierkegaard called the one who lives in true and yielding faith, is a lifelong quest, and the circle suggests a much more realistic story than our stories of progress that are shaped in an ascending line receding into the distance, or our stories of despair that end with some

The Hero's Journey

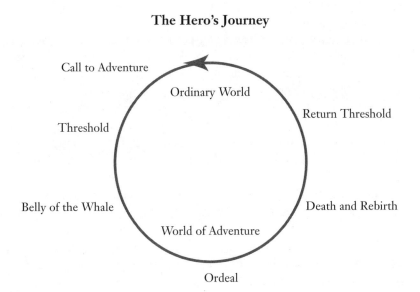

finality in a tangle. We may be called into confusion many times in our lives, and our response to it will determine whether we grow or diminish.

Life is shaped of loss, from the moment we leave the warm darkness of the womb and enter this bright loud world. Everything changes, even if we want it to stand still, even if we believe it *is* standing still. We lose our illusions, we lose possessions, we lose those who matter to us, we lose our physical capabilities, and, eventually, we lose our lives. Everything changes, and eventually, no matter who we are or how many toys we have, we will lose everything that is keyed to this physical world. It is how we deal with those losses that ultimately matters, and that is why without a resilient story that incorporates continuing change, we ourselves are lost.

And that should not—must not—happen in a universe established by a loving God. Review your stories for false premises and faulty plots; seek a story that incorporates suffering but encourages hope; stand alongside those who suffer, who grieve, whose stories have fallen apart. This is the good work that is given to us today in the only story that truly matters.

As with Campbell's idea of the hero's journey, Henri Nouwen argued that in the Christ-event, especially in the liturgical cycles that we celebrate as the universal church each year, every story that matters can be understood. In Advent, Christ is coming; in Lent, Christ is suffering; in Holy Week, Christ dies; in Easter, Christ is risen; in Pentecost, Christ sends his Spirit into the world. We can understand our experience through this circle of birth, suffering, death, rebirth, and service; it is, as Nouwen notes, "the only story ever told. It is the story from which all other stories receive their meaning and significance. The story of Christ makes history real."[5]

Whatever challenges may loom as we face suffering in this life, we serve a God of hope, a Christ who, as the Celts (and Nouwen) realized, has walked the path before us. And knowing that, hope and life can be placed into the story of suffering and death as its ultimate end, even if we cannot yet see how that might come. Jürgen Moltmann writes: "Wherever life is perceived and lived in community and fellowship with Christ, a new beginning is discovered in every end. What it is I do not know, but I have confidence that the new beginning will find me and raise me up."[6]

May this promise of new beginnings in every ending be strength for your journey.

Acknowledgments

This book is the product of some years of study, many years of hard living, and most specifically, a long summer spent working as a full-time chaplain in a busy urban trauma center. Many thanks to my Brackenridge Hospital mentor Pablo Holguin for showing me how to be a chaplain, and to the other staff chaplains I worked with and learned from, Frank and Enid. Thanks also to my fellow chaplain interns from the summer of 2006, particularly Steve Vittorini, Heath Abel, and Carissa Baldwin, and to the staff of the Seton CPE program for this opportunity to stand alongside great suffering and try to understand it.

This book is also the product of some audacity and anxiety, since everyone from Augustine on (up?) has asked these questions about sin, pain, and death. I hoped that a narrative approach and a willingness to sit with these stories and see where they take us might lead to some productive insights, and I think it has. But my debts are still obvious—without the writing, preaching, and scholarship of people such as Walter Brueggemann, Rowan Williams, Stanley Hauerwas, Barbara Brown Taylor, John Claypool, Thomas Merton, Henri Nouwen, and Joseph Campbell (to name a few), this project would be much less than it is.

Thanks also to my friends Chris Seay, Philip Newell, Scott Walker, Tom Hanks, Blake Burleson, Roger Paynter, Brian McLaren, Hunt Priest, Roger Joslin, Chad Vaughn, Cathy Boyd,

Ken Malcolm, Don Smith, Carissa Baldwin, Heath Abel, Joe Behen, and Elizabeth Anagnostis for theological and real-life conversations that had a bearing on this book, and to Martha Salazar for her love, generosity, wisdom, and ongoing support for my work.

It is a joy and a privilege to work with the publishing professionals at Westminster John Knox. Particular thanks go to my editor, David Dobson; my publicist, Emily Kiefer; and my editor at The Thoughtful Christian, David Maxwell. I'm also grateful to all the WJK staff—editorial, sales, and fulfillment—in the United States and United Kingdom who get my books out and into the hands of people like you.

Baylor University has been my teaching home for almost twenty years, and I have been supported by its administration whether I'm publishing fiction, memoir, or theology. As always, I'm grateful to Baylor provost Randall O'Brien; my dean, Lee Nordt; my former department chair, Maurice Hunt; and my current chair, Dianna Vitanza. Their willingness to let me formally study theology, to write what inspires me, and to teach a condensed schedule makes it possible for me to do the writing that is a chief part of my vocation. I am also grateful to my students at Baylor for conversations about story, suffering, and all the rest—I learn at least as much from them as they do from me.

Thanks to the Episcopal Theological Seminary of the Southwest in Austin, Texas, for training me, for giving me an ongoing place to write, and for a continuing community of faith and learning. I especially want to thank Tony Baker, Cynthia Briggs Kittredge, Ray Pickett, Steve Bishop, Russell Schultz, and Charlie Cook for meaningful conversations into and instruction about these matters, and Bob Kinney for expert help in publicizing what I write.

St. David's Episcopal Church in Austin, Texas, has become my faith home, the place where I worship, lead retreats, preach, and teach. Thanks to its rector David Boyd, to whom this book is dedicated, for inviting me to come to St. David's and serve, and to his staff, the Revs. Ken Malcolm, Ron Smith, Chad Vaughn, and Mary Vano. Thanks also to my former communities of faith, St. James Episcopal Church, Austin, and to the Revs. Hugh Craig,

Bill Adams, and Amy Donohue-Adams there, and to the good people of Calvary Episcopal Church, Bastrop, Texas, led by the Rev. Matt Zimmerman. Thanks to my former rector from St. James, the Rt. Rev. Greg Rickel, Bishop of Olympia, for his love and support, and for years of ongoing conversation.

Thanks also to those places where this book was written: the Episcopal Theological Seminary of the Southwest; Ghost Ranch, in Abiquiu, New Mexico; and the Cathedral College at the National Cathedral in Washington, D.C. At ETSS, I thank Alan Gregory and John Bennet Waters for that office where I write and read; at Ghost Ranch, my hosts were Carole Landess at the Casa del Sol retreat center, and my dear friend Jim Baird, Program Director; at the College, I am grateful to Wanda Rixon for arranging my 2007 visit as a College Reader, and to College Warden Howard Anderson, Associate Warden Shelagh Casey Brown, Dean McDonald, the head of the College of Preachers, and all the staff of that great institution for their hospitality and encouragement.

This book takes on great themes and walks into great darkness, but I intend that it will lead us in a singular direction toward some story that works, a story of light and hope. If there's one life-message I can condense from these pages, this might be it: love well, laugh often, and trust that the One who created us will not abandon us, now or ever.

It is that Holy One of Blessing that I thank most of all, for these words, for the opportunity to write them, and for the life that has been a gift beyond measure, in good times and in bad.

The Cathedral College of Preachers
Washington, DC
Advent 2007

Notes

Introduction

1. I have changed the names and some of the identifying details of all patients, family, and medical staff throughout the book to protect their privacy. I have, however, preserved essential details about their lives—ethnicity, family history, family dynamics, medical details, and so on—in the interest of presenting their stories as authentically as possible. With their permission, I have used the names of my fellow chaplains.
2. Harold S. Kushner, *When Bad Things Happen to Good People* (New York: Avon Books, 1981), 1.
3. Ibid., 2.
4. C. S. Lewis, *A Grief Observed* (1961; repr., New York: Bantam Books, 1976), 4–5.
5. Robin Griffith-Jones, *The Four Witnesses* (New York: HarperCollins, 2000), 352.
6. John Polkinghorne, *The God of Hope and the End of the World* (New Haven, CT: Yale University Press, 2002), 29.
7. Jürgen Moltmann, *The Source of Life: The Holy Spirit and the Theology of Life* (Minneapolis: Fortress Press, 1997), 81.
8. Lewis, *Grief Observed*, 80–81.
9. E. M. Forster, *Aspects of the Novel* (1927; repr., New York: Harvest, 1955), 86.
10. Ibid.,
11. Anne Lamott, *Traveling Mercies: Some Thoughts on Faith* (New York: Anchor Books, 2000), 67.

Chapter 1

1. For additional information on the Baylor survey, or to download its initial report, you may visit Baylor Institute for Studies of Religion, "American Piety in the 21st Century," http://www.baylor.edu/isreligion/index.php?id=40634.

123

2. John Dominic Crossan, "Opening Statement," *The Resurrection of Jesus: John Dominic Crossan and N. T. Wright in Dialogue*, ed. Robert B. Stewart (Minneapolis: Fortress Press, 2006), 28–29.

3. Stanley Hauerwas, *Naming the Silences: God, Medicine, and the Problem of Suffering* (Grand Rapids: Eerdmans, 1990), 140.

4. Anselm, "Proslogium," *St. Anselm: Basic Writings*, trans. S. N. Deane (Chicago: Open Court, 1994), 68.

5. Barbara Brown Taylor, *God in Pain* (Nashville: Abingdon Press, 1998), 20.

6. Marcus J. Borg and John Dominic Crossan, *The Last Week: What the Gospels Really Teach about Jesus's Final Days in Jerusalem* (New York: HarperSanFrancisco, 2006), 123.

7. John Claypool, *Tracks of a Fellow Struggler: Living and Growing through Grief*, rev. ed. (1974; New Orleans: Insight Press, 1995), 49, 54.

8. For an accessible historical and theological discussion of the evolution of Satan as a literary and spiritual force, see Elaine Pagels's *The Origin of Satan* (New York: Vintage Books, 1995).

9. Walter Wink, *Unmasking the Powers: The Invisible Forces That Determine Human Existence* (Philadelphia: Fortress Press, 1986), 1.

10. Augustine, *The City of God* xx.2.

11. Isa. 45:5–7; Lewis Jacobs, "Zoroastrianism," *A Concise Companion to the Jewish Religion*, Oxford University Press, 1999, *Oxford Reference Online*, http://www.oxfordreference.com/views/ENTRY.html?subview=Main&entry=t96.e798.

12. Jouette M. Bassler, "God in the NT," *Anchor Bible Dictionary*, vol. 2 (New York: Doubleday, 1992), 1049.

13. John J. Scullion, "God in the OT," *Anchor Bible Dictionary*, vol. 2 (New York: Doubleday, 1992), 1043–44.

14. Harold S. Kushner, *When Bad Things Happen to Good People* (New York: Avon Books, 1981), 3.

15. "My Own Personal Jesus," *Scrubs*, episode 1.11, 2003.

16. Augustine famously said, "Miracles are not contrary to nature, but only contrary to what we know about nature."

17. Thomas Aquinas, *A Summa of the* Summa, ed. Peter Kreeft (San Francisco: Ignatius Press, 1990), 105–6; 237–38.

18. Kushner, *When Bad Things Happen*, 29.

19. John J. Ó Ríordáin, *The Music of What Happens: Celtic Spirituality* (Dublin: Columba Press, 1996), 100.

20. Alexander Carmichael, *Carmina Gadelica: Hymns and Incantations Collected in the Highlands and Islands of Scotland in the Last Century*, ed. C. J. Moore (Edinburgh: Floris Books, 1992), 312.

21. J. Philip Newell, *One Foot in Eden: A Celtic View of the Stages of Life* (New York: Paulist Press, 1999), 88.

22. Rowan Williams, *Writing in the Dust: After September 11* (Grand Rapids: Eerdmans, 2002), 8.

23. David Ray Griffin, *God, Power, and Evil: A Process Theodicy* (Philadelphia: Westminster Press, 1976), 310.

24. Williams, *Writing in the Dust*, 8.

25. "Process theology," *The Concise Oxford Dictionary of World Religions*, ed. John Bowker, Oxford University Press, 2000, *Oxford Reference Online*, http://www.oxfordreference.com/views/ENTRY.html?subview=Main&entry=t101.e578.

26. The work of Jack Miles, including the Pulitzer Prize–winning *God: A Biography*, suggests that God is growing, learning, and evolving from his contacts with humankind—*in* process, if you will—a convincing explanation for the radically different characterizations of God to be found in the Scriptures.

27. Thomas Aquinas, *A Summa of the* Summa, 78–79.

28. Jürgen Moltmann, *The Crucified God: The Cross of Christ as the Foundation and Criticism of Christian Theology* (London: SCM Press, 1974), 190. Hans Urs von Balthasar argues that such accounts of the suffering God and of process theology in general may confuse the actions of the immanent Trinity (the essential relationship between the three persons of the Trinity) and the actions of the economic Trinity (how we perceive the workings of the Trinity in the process of human history). Perhaps; how am I to know what goes on between the persons of the Trinity? However, I present the teachings of Moltmann and of process theology to offer another "operative theology" worthy of exploration. Hans Urs von Balthasar, *Theo-Drama: Theological Dramatic Theory, Vol. IV: The Action*, trans. Graham Harrison (San Francisco: Ignatius Press, 1994), 324.

29. Desmond Tutu, *God Has a Dream: A Vision of Hope for Our Time* (New York: Doubleday, 2004), 15.

30. Ibid., 17.

31. Søren Kierkegaard, *Fear and Trembling*, trans. Alastair Hannay (1985; repr., New York: Penguin, 2006), 54.

Chapter 2

1. Alisdair McIntyre, *After Virtue: A Study in Moral Theory*, 2nd ed. (1981; South Bend, IN: University of Notre Dame Press, 1984), 216.

2. N. T. Wright, *Evil and the Justice of God* (Downers Grove, IL: IVP Books, 2006), 21–22.

3. Dan P. McAdams, *The Redemptive Self: Stories Americans Live By* (New York: Oxford University Press, 2006), 242.

4. Henri Nouwen, *Turn My Mourning into Dancing: Finding Hope in Hard Times*, ed. Timothy James (Nashville: W Publishing, 2001), 9.

5. H. Richard Niebuhr, *Radical Monotheism and Western Culture* (1960; repr., Louisville, KY: Westminster John Knox Press, 1993), 21.

6. Ibid., passim.

7. Benjamin Franklin, *Autobiography and Other Writings*, ed. Kenneth Silverman (New York: Penguin Books, 1986), 3.

8. McIntyre, *After Virtue*, 213.

9. Barbara Brown Taylor, *God in Pain: Teaching Sermons on Suffering* (Nashville: Abingdon Press, 1998), 120–21.

10. P. D. James, *The Children of Men* (1992; repr., New York: Vintage Books, 2006), 5.

11. Stanley Hauerwas, *Naming the Silences: God, Medicine, and the Problem of Suffering* (Grand Rapids: Eerdmans, 1990), 35.

12. Ibid., 71.

13. Dan Bagby, e-mail interview, April 11, 2005.

14. Hauerwas, *Naming the Silences*, 125.

15. John Polkinghorne, *The God of Hope and the End of the World* (New Haven, CT: Yale University Press, 2002), 40.

16. Hauerwas, *Naming the Silences*, 125.

17. Thomas Merton, *Conjectures of a Guilty Bystander* (New York: Image, 1968), 47.

18. To be completely accurate, Jared Diamond lumps together "North America, Western Europe, Japan, and Australia" in the group of developed nations that, per capita, consume thirty-two times more goods and services than does an individual in the developing world ("What's Your Consumption Factor?" *New York Times*, Jan. 2, 2008, http://www.nytimes.com/2008/01/02/opinion/02diamond.html?pagewanted=1&ei=5087&em&en=4db8384a792991d6&ex=1199595600).

19. "In Place of God," *The Economist*, May 3, 2007, http://economist.com/surveys/displaystory.cfm?story_id=9070673.

20. Which makes the expectation of many American Christians for earthly wealth as well as spiritual gifts problematic. See David van Biema and Jeff Chu's *Time* cover article "Does God Want You to Be Rich?" for a balanced discussion of the so-called Prosperity Gospel, *Time*, Sept. 10, 2006, http://www.time.com/time/magazine/article/0,9171,1533448,00.html.

21. Merton, *Conjectures of a Guilty Bystander*, 98.

22. Julie Appleby, "Debate Surrounds End-of-Life Health Care Costs," *USA Today*, Oct. 19, 2006, http://www.usatoday.com/money/industries/health/2006-10-18-end-of-life-costs_x.htm.

23. I love the revision to this practice my friend the Rev. Amy Donohue-Adams has managed to institute at the hospital where she is chaplain: "AND" (Allow Natural Death). This seems to me a much more positive view of death than a failure to resuscitate.

24. Karl Rahner and Herbert Vorgrimler, *Dictionary of Theology*, 2nd ed. (New York: Crossroad, 1981), 401–2.

25. Henri J. M. Nouwen, *Finding My Way Home: Pathways to Life and the Spirit* (New York: Crossroad, 2001), 33, 29.

26. Jack Miles, *Christ: A Crisis in the Life of God* (New York: Vintage Books, 2001), 207 and passim.

27. Jim Wallis, "Dangerous Religion: George W. Bush's Theology of Empire," *Mississippi Review* vol. 10, no. 1 (2004), http://www.mississippireview.com/2004/Vol10No1-Jan04/1001–0104-wallis.html.

28. Nouwen, *Finding My Way Home*, 101.

29. Henri Nouwen, *The Selfless Way of Christ: Downward Mobility and the Spiritual Life* (Maryknoll, NY: Orbis Books, 2007), 34–35.

30. Ernest Hemingway, "A Clean, Well-Lighted Place," in *The Complete Short Stories of Ernest Hemingway* (1987; repr., New York: Scribner's, 2003), 291.

31. Stephen Crane, "A man said to the universe," in *Oxford Anthology of American Literature*, ed. William Rose Benét and Norman Holmes Pearson (New York: Oxford University Press, 1938), 1009.

32. Stephen Crane, "The Open Boat," in *The Art of the Short Story*, ed. Dana Gioia and R. S. Gwynn (New York: Longman, 2006), 207.

Chapter 3

1. In a recent speech at my seminary, Jewish scholar Amy-Jill Levine remarked that she prefers "Old Testament" instead of "Hebrew Bible" or other such constructions. Since she's Jewish, no one will be offended if she says so; since I'm a Christian scholar, I'll continue to use "Hebrew Testament," "Hebrew Bible," and "Hebrew Scriptures," in these pages, since those terms avoid any suggestion on my part that the Christian Testament somehow nullifies or supersedes God's covenant with the Jews.

2. Bernhard W. Anderson and Steven Bishop, *Out of the Depths: The Psalms Speak for Us Today*, 3rd ed. (Louisville, KY: Westminster John Knox Press, 2000), 49, 60.

3. Ibid., 51.

4. Erich Zenger, *A God of Vengeance? Understanding the Psalms of Divine Wrath*, trans. Linda M. Maloney (Louisville, KY: Westminster John Knox Press, 1996), 73; Anderson and Bishop, *Out of the Depths*, 74.

5. Some of the apocryphal books that precede the New Testament, like Maccabees, resonate with the idea of the righteous martyr, the person who is faithful and who will be rewarded in the next life. But these laments we're examining in Psalms (and by extension elsewhere in the Hebrew Bible) do not look to the next life for wrongs to be righted.

6. Anderson and Bishop, *Out of the Depths*, 60.

7. Dietrich Bonhoeffer, *Psalms: The Prayer Book of the Bible*, trans. James H. Burtness (Minneapolis: Augsburg, 1974), 47.

8. Walter Brueggemann, *The Message of the Psalms* (Minneapolis: Augsburg, 1984), 11.

9. Ibid., 21, and passim.

10. Ibid., 114.

11. This real-life story from Wiesel's past is the basis for his play *The Trial of God*, set in 1649 in the midst of pogroms against the Jews.

12. Brueggemann, *Message of the Psalms*, 52.
13. Anderson and Bishop, *Out of the Depths*, 60.
14. F. W. Dobbs-Allsopp, *Lamentations* (Louisville, KY: Westminster John Knox Press, 2002), 28.
15. Stephen Mitchell, *The Book of Job* (San Francisco: North Point Press, 1987), 6.
16. Harold S. Kushner, *When Bad Things Happen to Good People* (New York: Avon Books, 1981), 37.
17. Marvin H. Pope, *Job*, Anchor Bible (Garden City, NY: Doubleday, 1965), xiii.
18. Ibid., lxxv.
19. Mitchell, *Book of Job*, xxix.
20. Ibid., xix; J. H. Wheaton, *Job* (1985; repr., London: T & T Clark, 2004), 50.
21. Thomas Merton, *No Man Is an Island* (1955; repr., New York: Harvest, 1983), 17.
22. Kushner, *When Bad Things Happen*, 43.
23. Brueggemann, *Message of the Psalms*, 113.

Chapter 4

1. Søren Kierkegaard, *The Sickness unto Death*, trans. Walter Lowrie (Princeton, NJ: Princeton University Press, 1941), 24.
2. Barbara Brown Taylor, *God in Pain: Teaching Sermons on Suffering* (Nashville: Abingdon Press, 1998), 57.
3. Thomas Lynch, "Good Grief: An Undertaker's Reflections," *Christian Century*, July 26, 2003, 20.
4. Thomas Merton, *No Man Is an Island* (1955; repr., New York: Harvest, 1983), 23.
5. Rudolf Bultmann, *The Gospel of John: A Commentary*, trans. G. R. Beasley-Murray et al. (Philadelphia: Westminster Press, 1971), 407.
6. Cynthia Briggs Kittredge, *Conversations with Scripture: The Gospel of John* (Harrisburg, PA: Morehouse, 2007), 57.
7. Robin Griffith-Jones, *The Four Witnesses* (New York: HarperSanFranscisco, 2000), 353.
8. Merton, *No Man Is an Island*, 17.
9. Rowan Williams, *Resurrection: Interpreting the Easter Gospel*, rev. ed. (Cleveland: Pilgrim Press, 2002), 17.
10. Rowan Williams, *On Christian Theology* (Oxford: Wiley-Blackwell, 2000), 186.
11. Desmond Tutu, *God Has a Dream: A Vision of Hope for Our Time* (New York: Doubleday, 2004), 66.
12. Jürgen Moltmann, *The Coming of God: Christian Eschatology*, trans. Margaret Kohl (Minneapolis: Fortress Press, 1996), xi.
13. John Polkinghorne, *The God of Hope and the End of the World* (New Haven, CT: Yale University Press, 2002), 102.

Chapter 5

1. Barbara Brown Taylor, *God in Pain: Teaching Sermons on Suffering* (Nashville: Abingdon Press, 1998), 59.
2. John Claypool, *Tracks of a Fellow Struggler: Living and Growing through Grief*, rev. ed. (1974; New Orleans: Insight Press, 1995), 94.
3. Henri Nouwen, *Turn My Mourning into Dancing: Finding Hope in Hard Times*, ed. Timothy Jones (Nashville: W Publishing, 2001), 17, 53.
4. Claypool, *Tracks of a Fellow Struggler*, 35–37.
5. *The Book of Common Prayer* (New York: Oxford University Press, 1990), 464.
6. Thomas Lynch, "Good Grief: An Undertaker's Reflections," *Christian Century*, July 23, 2003, 20.
7. Greg Garrett, *Crossing Myself* (Colorado Springs: NavPress, 2006), 13–14.
8. Thomas Merton, *No Man Is an Island* (1955; repr., New York: Harvest, 1983), 17.
9. Jürgen Moltmann, *The Spirit of Life: A Universal Affirmation* (1992; repr., Minneapolis: Fortress Press, 2001), 114.

Conclusion

1. Joseph Campbell, *The Hero with a Thousand Faces* (1949; repr., Princeton, NJ: Princeton University Press, 1968), 58.
2. This recap is a simplified summary I've created from years of teaching and writing about the archetypal story; I believe it is faithful to that narrative, and somewhat easier to follow than other versions. My sources: Joseph Campbell, *The Hero with a Thousand Faces*; Joseph Campbell with Bill Moyers, *The Power of Myth*, ed. Betty Sue Flowers (New York: Anchor Books, 1991); Christopher Vogler, *The Writer's Journey: Mythic Structure for Writers*, 3rd ed. (Studio City, CA: Michael Wiese Productions, 2007).
3. Campbell, *Power of Myth*, 80.
4. Ibid., 151, 154–55.
5. Henri Nouwen, *The Selfless Way of Christ: Downward Mobility and the Spiritual Life* (Maryknoll, NY: Orbis Books, 2007), 75.
6. Jürgen Moltmann, *The Coming of God: Christian Eschatology*, trans. Margaret Kohl (Minneapolis: Fortress Press, 1996), xi.

About the Author

Greg Garrett is the author of nonfiction works focusing on theology and narrative including *The Gospel according to Hollywood*, *The Gospel Reloaded* (with Chris Seay), and *Holy Superheroes;* of the critically acclaimed novels *Free Bird* (named by *Publishers Weekly* and the *Denver Rocky Mountain News* as one of the best first novels of 2002) and *Cycling*, and the forthcoming novel *Shame*; of the memoirs *Crossing Myself* and the forthcoming *No Idea*; and of a number of books of the Bible for *The Voice* Scripture project. He has written on narrative, culture, religion, and politics for print and Web publications including *Poets & Writers*, *Christianity Today*, *Utne*, *Relevant*, *Ethics Daily*, and The Thoughtful Christian, and he blogs for *The Christian Century* at theotherjesus.com. Professor of English at Baylor University, where he has twice received university-wide teaching honors, he serves the Episcopal Theological Seminary of the Southwest as Writer in Residence, and also regularly teaches, gives readings, lectures, and leads workshops and retreats across the United States and overseas. Greg is a lay preacher at St. David's Episcopal Church in Austin, Texas, where he lives with his sons Jake and Chandler.